In Flanders Fields
By John McCrae

In Flanders fields the poppies blow
Between the crosses, row on row,
That mark our place; and in the sky
The larks, still bravely singing, fly
Scarce heard amid the guns below.

We are the Dead. Short days ago
We lived, felt dawn, saw sunset glow,
Loved and were loved, and now we lie,
In Flanders fields.

Take up our quarrel with the foe:
To you from failing hands we throw
The torch; be yours to hold it high.
If ye break faith with us who die
We shall not sleep, though poppies grow
In Flanders fields.

WHISTLE STOP Café MYSTERIES

Under the Apple Tree
As Time Goes By
We'll Meet Again
Till Then
I'll Be Seeing You
Fools Rush In

FOOLS
RUSH IN

BETH ADAMS

Whistle Stop Café Mysteries is a trademark of Guideposts.

Published by Guideposts Books & Inspirational Media
100 Reserve Road, Suite E200
Danbury, CT 06810
Guideposts.org

Cover and interior design by Müllerhaus
Cover illustration by Greg Copeland at Illustration Online, LLC.
Typeset by Aptara, Inc.

ISBN 978-1-961125-03-2 (hardcover)
ISBN 978-1-961125-05-6 (epub)

Printed and bound in the United States of America
10 9 8 7 6 5 4 3 2 1

FOOLS
RUSH IN

CHAPTER ONE

The sky was dark velvet, pricked with spots of golden light. Dawn was still more than an hour away, and the air was crisp and cold. *Fall is here, there's no doubt about that,* Janet Shaw thought as she walked down the steps and into the kitchen. Her husband, Ian, was still asleep and would be for hours. She filled Ranger's bowl with cat food and refilled Laddie's water dish, pulled on her coat, and stepped outside. The neighborhood was quiet, the streets still. Janet loved this time of day, when the world was silent and it felt like it belonged just to her.

She started the car, and the engine hummed. She flipped on her lights and looked around, and then she backed out of the driveway as the air inside the car started to warm. It wasn't a long drive to the Whistle Stop Café, but walking it at this hour would be asking a bit too much.

The car was making a weird banging noise. Ian had promised to take a look at it but hadn't had the chance. For now, she ignored it, and as she drove through the sleepy streets of the small town of Dennison, she made a mental list of the game plan for the day. She'd get the pie-crusts made and chilling first, and then she'd turn her attention to the day's other baked goods. She was thinking cranberry and white chocolate for the scones, plus the traditional plain and blueberry. And some pumpkin spice muffins were in order—those would sell well on a crisp fall day like today. Oh, and she could make apple cinnamon too, topped with a sugar and cinnamon crumble. She would make a batch of doughnuts as well… She was getting hungry just thinking about them. But first, coffee. She'd get that started as soon as she got in. Caffeine made the early mornings bearable.

Janet would never stop being grateful she'd been able to open the Whistle Stop Café with her best friend, Debbie Albright, in the old train depot. Janet had worked in a bakery in Uhrichsville for years, but owning a business with Debbie was a dream come true. They'd been doing great since they launched this past summer, and had already developed a steady stream of loyal customers.

Janet parked the car and walked up to the old train depot. It appeared a murky brown in the dim predawn light but was actually a vintage redbrick and stone structure. The café was at the west end of the building, and she started toward it—

But wait. Why was a light on inside? It looked bright and cheerful, casting the interior of the café in a warm glow, but Janet knew this was a big problem. There shouldn't be any lights on in the café at this hour. She walked faster. Had they left them on when they'd closed down yesterday? She didn't think so. Someone would have noticed before now, wouldn't they? But was it possible—

She stopped short. The door was open. She and Debbie definitely hadn't left the door open. And there was something shiny on the ground at the base of the door. Was that—

She stifled a shriek when she saw that the glinting was the light from inside being reflected on broken glass. The glass that used to be part of the door.

Should she go in? But what if whoever had done this was still there? No way. She wasn't going in there. Not alone, anyway. Janet pulled out her phone and dialed quickly.

"Hello?" Ian's voice was groggy.

"Ian?" Janet's husband was the local chief of police.

"Janet? What's going on?" Now Ian was on full alert.

"I think someone broke into the café. The door is open, the light is on, and there's glass on the ground. I'm afraid to go in there."

"Stay outside," he said. She could hear him moving around. "Don't go in, and don't hang up. I'm staying on the line, and I'll be right there."

Janet held her phone to her ear, staring at the café, trying to make sense of what she was seeing. So many people in town seemed delighted to have the old depot open and serving food again, just like it had all those decades ago. Who would do something like this? She bit her lip, trying to stay calm.

A few minutes later, headlights swept around the corner, and Ian parked his car and jumped out. He must have sped the whole way, but she was glad he'd come so quickly. She realized she was shaking.

"Are you okay?" Ian asked, walking toward her.

"I'm fine," Janet said. "I didn't go inside."

"I'll check it out. You stay here until I tell you it's clear." Ian walked to the café and pushed the door open with his toe. It scraped across the broken glass on the ground, but it opened. He edged his way in, on high alert, and peered around the café's dining area, behind the counter, and into the kitchen. After a moment Janet saw him come out of the café and go through the doors that led to the museum section of the depot. Then, finally, he came back out.

"It's clear. You can come in, but don't touch anything."

Janet stepped through the open door and bit back a cry. It was even worse than it had looked from outside. Several tables were overturned, tossed carelessly on top of one another. More than one chair leg was broken. But that wasn't the worst part. The worst was that the walls—the walls they had so lovingly painted a sunny yellow and hung with vintage photos of the depot in its heyday—had been covered with ugly red spray paint. Someone had painted zigzags and other random designs all over the walls and even over the pictures. And—oh my. One of the pictures was missing, and a spray-painted crown had been left in its place.

"They tried to break into this," Ian said. He stood over the cash register, shining a flashlight at the edge. Janet went over and saw that he was pointing at a place where the paint had been scraped away. "It doesn't look like they succeeded."

"I'm glad of that," Janet said. "Though there's nothing in it. We empty it and put the cash in the safe every day when we close." Thank goodness. At least they hadn't lost hundreds of dollars on top of whatever it was going to cost to get this place fixed up. Insurance would cover at least some of it, she hoped.

"Where's the safe?" Ian asked.

"It's in the back."

"Why don't you go check to make sure it's still locked. Just don't touch it."

"I won't." Janet hurried to the kitchen to where the safe was tucked under a counter. She was relieved to see that it was closed. Only she and Debbie knew the combination. She walked back into the café. "They didn't get into it," she said.

Ian nodded. He used his phone to take a picture of the marks on the cash register. "That's good to hear."

Janet heard sirens, and a moment later a Dennison Police Department cruiser came blazing into the parking lot, its blue and red lights strobing in the predawn gloom. When had Ian called the station? Deputy Brendan Vaughn stepped out of the vehicle and rushed into the café. He was tall and had close-cropped brown hair.

"Good work getting here so quickly," Ian said to him. "Looks like someone was hoping for a quick payday." He gestured toward the cash register. "They didn't get anything though."

"That's good news," Deputy Vaughn said. "Should I start dusting for prints?"

Brendan Vaughn was only a few years out of the police academy and looked like he spent a lot of time at the gym. Janet knew several single women in town who had their eye on him.

"It probably won't do much good, with how many people are in and out of this place every day, but you might as well try," Ian said. "I'll photograph the scene."

While Ian and his deputy got to work, Janet called Debbie. It was earlier than she normally got up, but she would want to know what was going on.

"Hi. What's wrong?" Debbie sounded groggy.

"Someone broke into the café." Janet nearly choked on the words.

"What do you mean? Is everything okay?"

"They tried to get the register open but weren't able to. They broke the glass on the door and turned the tables and chairs over and spray-painted the walls."

"I'll be right there."

"Okay. Ian and Deputy Vaughn are here, but I figured you'd want to know right away."

"You figured right. I'll see you in a few."

Janet tried to stay out of the way as she waited for Debbie. She wandered over to the dining area and started to pick up a table, but Ian called out, "Don't touch that yet!"

She'd have to wait to clean up. "Can I at least start the coffee?"

"Let us finish up back here," Ian said from behind the counter. He was taking pictures of everything while Deputy Vaughn dusted a fine black powder all over the cash register. "We'll be done soon."

Janet stood in the dining room and looked up at the spot on the back wall where the crown had been spray-painted. What was that about? The picture that had hung there was one of her favorites. It was a black-and-white shot taken sometime in the early '40s, when the space that was now the café had been a canteen that provided hot meals and baked goods, especially doughnuts, to the servicemen and women passing through on military transport trains. The picture showed three women standing behind a table set in the grassy area in front of the depot. There was a briefcase on the table, an old-fashioned one with hard sides and a handle. It was a charming picture that depicted the station when it was a stop on the route of many travelers. Janet and Debbie had chosen it, along with the other historic photos that lined the walls, from the collection housed in the depot's museum.

Ian moved from behind the counter to join Janet and take several pictures of the crown.

"It's a weird thing to paint there, isn't it?" Janet asked. None of the other graffiti portrayed a picture, at least not one she could recognize.

Ian didn't say anything but continued to photograph it. Then he moved to the door, where Deputy Vaughn dabbed at a shard of glass that was still attached to the doorframe.

"Looks like blood," Deputy Vaughn said quietly. He slid the sample into a sterile evidence bag.

"They must've gotten cut when they broke the glass," Ian said.

"That's my guess." Deputy Vaughn glanced up, saw that Janet was watching them, and muttered something to Ian.

In response, Ian said something under his breath, and the deputy nodded and responded. They obviously didn't want her to overhear. Janet stepped closer.

"...like the auto parts store," she heard Deputy Vaughn say.

"And Smollen got out last week," Ian said in reply. "We may need to pay him a visit."

Just then, Debbie came rushing into the café. She wore a gray sweater over a pair of baggy jeans, her coat flaps flying behind her.

"Oh my," she said as she stopped short inside the open door. "Oh, this is bad."

"It'll be all right," Janet said, hoping she sounded more optimistic than she felt. "It's not as bad as it could be."

Debbie had tears in her eyes as she looked from the tables to the graffiti to the glass on the ground. "Who did this?"

"We don't know yet," Ian said. "But we're going to find out."

CHAPTER TWO

While Ian and Deputy Vaughn finished taking pictures of the scene and dusting for prints, Debbie took photos of the mess with her phone for their insurance claim. Then Ian finally gave Janet permission to make a pot of coffee. While it brewed, Debbie made a sign that said CLOSED FOR REPAIRS from an old cardboard box and a black marker. Janet would have laughed if she hadn't wanted to cry so badly. They needed more than repairs.

Then, coffee in hand, Ian led Debbie and Janet toward the seating area, flipped a table back over, set four chairs upright, pulled them to the table, and gestured for them to have a seat.

"I need to take your statements," he said.

"Here?" Debbie seemed uncertain.

"Unless you'd rather come down to the station," Ian said. "I figure the sooner we get this done, the sooner you can start cleaning up."

Debbie looked over at Janet, who nodded. "Let's just do it here," she said, and Debbie agreed and took a seat across from Janet. Ian and Deputy Vaughn sat across from each other.

"Can you tell me what happened this morning?" Ian asked Janet.

Janet felt silly retelling the story, since she'd called him immediately and he'd been there for most of it. Still, as she drank her coffee, she went over the events of the morning so he could write up his statement, and then he asked Debbie to do the same.

"Can either of you think of anyone who might have had reason to break into the café?" Ian asked when Debbie finished.

Janet wanted to laugh. They were two middle-aged women who served customers and sold baked goods out of a historic railroad canteen in Ohio. They weren't exactly the type to have violent enemies. But just as she was about to tell Ian how silly his question was, Debbie spoke up.

"What about Alyssa?"

"Alyssa?" It took a moment for Janet to register the name. "Oh, Alyssa Brown, from Glazed?"

Glazed was the new doughnut shop in Uhrichsville that had recently opened in the space where Third Street Bakery used to be. The Whipples, who had owned Third Street Bakery, retired around the time Janet left, and the space sat empty for a few months until Alyssa Brown leased it to open her own shop. Alyssa was in her late twenties and specialized in doughnuts in flavors that sounded bizarre to Janet, like chai and chili pepper, matcha, and tres leches with clementine glaze. Janet had been dubious that Alyssa would find a market for flavors like those in small-town Ohio, but so far, she seemed to be doing all right. From what Janet heard, the shop had started to gain something of a cult following.

"They have the best red velvet doughnuts," Deputy Vaughn said, and then held up his hands. "I mean, I prefer your baking, of course."

Janet smiled at him. "That's okay," she said.

"Why do you think Alyssa might have been involved?" Ian asked.

"Because she's been…weird," Debbie said.

"What do you mean?" Ian asked.

"Well, Alyssa has come by the café, what, three times in the past couple of weeks?"

Janet nodded. "And each time, she's made a comment about how she wishes we weren't in business."

"She said she wishes you weren't in business?" Ian's eyes narrowed.

"Not in so many words," Debbie said. "She's more subtle than that. She'll say things like, 'Watch out, you guys are my biggest competition,' or 'I need to find a way to put you out of business,' but, like, laughing, so it seems like she's joking."

"But she's not," Janet added. "You can tell she means it."

"The last time, it was more than that," Debbie said. "She said the best thing that could happen for Glazed is if something bad happened to the Whistle Stop."

"She used those words?" Ian's eyes widened.

"She said it like it was a joke, like she was paying us a big compliment," Debbie said. "But it was weird."

"I think she's just insecure and trying to make sure her business stays afloat," Janet said.

"Is Glazed struggling?" Ian asked.

"I don't know," Janet admitted.

"Janet and I talked about Alyssa's comments and decided to ignore them," Debbie said. "But now that this has happened…"

"It's a big jump from making weird comments to breaking in and vandalizing our café," Janet said. "I get that, and I would hate to accuse her if she had nothing to do with it, but if you're asking whether anyone comes to mind, we can't just ignore what she's said."

"Don't forget robbing us," Debbie said, gesturing to the spot where the picture used to be. "Breaking in and vandalizing our café and robbing us."

"Right. That too," Janet said.

"It's worth looking into," Ian said. "Is there anyone else?"

"This may be crazy, but could it be related to that newspaper article?" Janet asked.

"The Cleveland *Plain Dealer* story?" Ian cocked his head.

They had been really excited to be featured in an article in the big-city paper about the five best new things to see and do in Ohio this fall. The short piece raved about Janet's baking as well as how they'd preserved the history of the canteen. The article featured a picture of Janet and Debbie wearing their aprons inside the café. "What could that have to do with it?" Deputy Vaughn asked.

"I'm not really sure," Janet said. "But if we're thinking Alyssa could be a suspect because of jealousy, maybe there's someone else who might be jealous too."

"I guess it's possible," Debbie said. "But I couldn't tell you who."

"Me neither. Everyone has been so kind and excited for us."

Ian shrugged. "Honestly, all signs point to this being a simple attempted burglary, but we'll look into every possibility."

"Are there security cameras here?" Deputy Vaughn asked.

"Yes," Debbie said. "There's a wireless camera right by the door. And Kim had some installed around the museum a few months back." The depot museum was at the other end of the building, separated from the café by what was once the large, open waiting area of the depot, and was full of artifacts and historical documents showcasing the history of the station.

"The camera by the door was smashed," Ian said. "I saw it on the way in."

"It was?" How had Janet missed that?

"It might have captured an image of the perpetrator before it was destroyed," Ian said. "Can I take a look?"

Janet handed him her phone. When he'd installed the camera a few months ago, he'd shown her how to check the video in the app. The camera only recorded when something came into its view, so it wouldn't be that hard to find the footage. Ian scrolled through the images on the phone and then shook his head. "All you can see is an object coming toward it before the camera shatters."

"That's too bad," Janet said.

"We'll see if the museum's cameras caught anything," Ian said.

"Is there anything else either of you can think of?" Deputy Vaughn asked.

"No." Janet was still so bewildered that this had happened. Debbie echoed her.

"In that case, we'll head down to the station and get this into the system," Ian said, shoving his chair back and standing. "We'll see if any fingerprints turn up a suspect, and we'll start looking into a few possibilities."

"Thank you." Janet stood up too, and then she leaned in and wrapped her arms around Ian. He pulled her close and held her. In this moment, he wasn't Ian Shaw, Police Chief. He was just her husband, and Janet felt her body relax against his. Ian would find out who had done this. Ian would keep them safe.

Deputy Vaughn stood and started flipping tables and chairs upright. Bless him. Before they walked out the door, he and Ian had set all the tables back where they belonged and swept up the glass on the floor.

"You should call someone to get this door fixed right away," Ian said. "Maybe call Greg."

"I'll do that this morning," Debbie said. Greg Connor had done some work on Debbie's house when she'd moved back to town, and his mother Paulette worked at the café part-time. "If he can't fix it, he'll know who can."

"Great." Ian gave Janet a kiss before heading out the door. "Let me know if you need anything. And don't worry. We'll find who did this."

Janet sure hoped he was right. She watched as they walked back to their cars. The sun was fully up now, and soon customers would start coming in.

"We don't have any fresh baked goods, but we could serve coffee to go," Janet said. That way they wouldn't disappoint their regulars, and they might be able to salvage a bit of income from this terrible morning.

"I think that's a good idea," Debbie said. "Do you think Greg's up?"

"He's got kids to get off to school. I'm sure he is."

"I'll go give him a call," Debbie said.

"Thanks." Janet refilled her coffee. "In the meantime, I'm starving. I'll go make us some eggs and toast." She wouldn't be doing her usual baking this morning, but they still needed to eat.

"That sounds great," Debbie said.

A few minutes later, Janet came out of the kitchen carrying plates of scrambled eggs and wheat toast slathered in butter.

"Bless you." Debbie took one of the plates and set it down on the closest table. "This looks delicious."

"Did you get ahold of Greg?"

"Yes, he's on his way. He'll be here soon." She picked up her fork. "I also made coffee for Patricia and Ashling. And Harry and Crosby should be by soon."

Harry Franklin worked at the depot as a porter back in its heyday, and he ate breakfast every morning at the café with his dog, Crosby. Patricia, Harry's granddaughter and a local attorney, met him there as often as she could for a peppermint mocha. Ashling Kelly was a recent high school graduate who always ordered a cake doughnut with chocolate frosting and a coffee with lots of room for cream and sugar.

"Patricia and Ashling were sad to see what happened. Patricia gave a seriously large tip." Debbie pointed to the tip jar, where Janet saw a ten and two fives.

"That was nice of her."

"She said she hoped it would help get the café open again soon."

Sometimes Janet couldn't believe how lucky she was to live in a town like Dennison, full of kind people who looked after one another.

Janet and Debbie chatted about the needed repairs as they ate, and a few minutes later, Greg arrived. He restored old houses for a living, and he was skilled at all kinds of handyman jobs.

"Wow," he said, looking around at the broken glass in the door and the red spray paint on the walls and pictures. "I'm so sorry this happened."

"Thank you for coming so quickly," Janet said. "As you can see, we have a bit of a mess to clean up."

"I can see that, all right," Greg said. "But it seems like your first issue is security." He gestured at the door. "You won't be able to lock up until we get this taken care of."

"How long does it take to replace a door?" Debbie asked.

"I'd need to order a new one if we decide to replace the whole thing," he said. "That could take weeks." He went to the door and swung it on its hinges. "But I don't see any reason to do that. We really only need to replace the window. I could get the glass cut in a day or two, probably. Maybe another day or so if you want safety glass, which would be harder to break."

"That would be great," Janet said. That was a lot better than waiting weeks and paying for a whole door. "We'll take the safety glass."

"I'll go down to the hardware store and get some plywood to cover the hole in the meantime. It won't be pretty, but it will secure the door, at least until we can get the glass replaced."

"Thank you," Debbie said. "That would mean we don't have to sleep here until we get it fixed, which would be nice."

Greg laughed. "You definitely should not do that." He continued to look around the room. "You'll also want to get those walls repainted as soon as possible. I can't do it today, but I could get Jaxon to come over and get started after he gets out of school."

"He would be willing to do that?" Janet asked. Greg's older son was a freshman at the local high school, and in Janet's interactions with him, he seemed like a nice kid. Greg was raising his two sons, Jaxon and Julian, after losing his wife to cancer five years ago.

"He doesn't have anything going on today that I know of, and he likes making extra money. I can send him over this afternoon. Do you know the name of the color of your paint?"

"Lemon Sorbet," Janet said. They had chosen it because it was the closest to the canteen's original color.

"All right, then," Greg said. "I'll head over to the hardware store now and be back shortly to get started on this door."

"Thanks so much," Janet said.

Once he was gone, Debbie turned to her. "I'll go call the insurance company."

"Thank you." There was nothing Janet wanted to do less than deal with the insurance company. Debbie, who'd left a high-powered job in Cleveland to move home to Dennison, was probably better suited to the task.

In the meantime, Janet decided to do a little baking, even if they couldn't fully open the café today. By the time Debbie was off the phone, Greg was back and installing a piece of plywood over the broken glass and Janet was carrying a plate of freshly baked chocolate cookies out of the kitchen.

"Those smell delicious," Debbie said.

"I figured we needed a little bit of pure comfort food today." Janet set the plate down and invited Greg and Debbie to help themselves. She picked one up and took a bite. It was warm and sweet and packed with butter and melted chocolate. It was exactly what she needed.

Greg finished up with the door and promised to send Jaxon over after school to start on the walls. Janet and Debbie thanked him, and after he left, Janet turned to Debbie.

"How did it go with the insurance company?"

"It wasn't my favorite thing I've ever done," Debbie said. She sat down at the table with the cookies and helped herself to another. "But the woman I spoke with was nice enough. It sounds like they'll cover the full cost of repairs."

"That's good." Janet picked up another cookie and took a bite. While she chewed, she reflected on what had happened. "It's so weird, isn't it?"

"The break-in?"

"The break-in, and the fact that it seems to have been an attempted theft, but the only thing they ended up taking was an old picture."

"It was good that they couldn't get the cash register open," Debbie said. "And apparently didn't know about the safe."

"That's true. But even if the thief was disappointed about not being able to get into the register, why take a picture off the wall?"

"Maybe they thought it was better to leave with something rather than nothing," Debbie suggested. "Maybe they took it out of frustration."

"But why that one?" The photo had been hanging on the wall farthest from the door. "Why not take one closer to the door, if you're just going to grab a random photo off the wall?"

"And why spray-paint over the ones you leave behind?" Debbie gestured at the other photos on the walls, several of which had paint on them. "I don't pretend to understand the mind of a thief. Maybe whoever did this really liked that picture for some reason."

"You think they wanted to do some redecorating?" Janet asked, raising an eyebrow, "and found something that would look nice on their wall?"

"No, that probably wasn't it," Debbie said, laughing. "I don't know. It had to have just been random."

"It was one of my favorite pictures," Janet said. "The three women were all smiling, having a good time, and I've always wondered what the briefcase was for."

"Maybe Kim would be able to help us replace the picture," Debbie said. "Was that the only copy of the photo?"

"No," Janet said. "It was just a high-quality scan. The original is still in the museum's archives."

"Well, there you go," Debbie said. "Insurance will replace the frame, and we'll get another copy of the photo. Soon this place will be as good as new."

"In the meantime, we could get started cleaning off the other pictures," Janet said.

"Do you think we'll be able to get the paint off? I was thinking we'd need to buy new frames."

"Vinegar or rubbing alcohol might work. Let's try that first before we go out and spend more money. We should take the pictures out of the frames first, though, in case of leaks."

"Sounds good."

They carefully removed the prints from the frames and got to work. Janet was pleased to see that vinegar actually did strip off the spray paint. She was lost in her thoughts, focusing on the task at hand, when she realized her phone was ringing. Where had she left it? She looked around and found it on the counter. DAD, read the screen.

"Hello? Dad?" He'd probably heard about the break-in and was calling to make sure she was all right.

"Hi, Janet. Can you hear me?"

"Dad, why are you whispering?"

"I'm in the bathroom. Your mother is in the kitchen, and I don't want her to hear me."

"Is that the shower running?"

"She thinks I'm taking a shower."

"Dad, what's going on?" Janet's parents lived in town, and she saw and spoke with them regularly. But it was unlike her father to call her like this. "Is everything okay?"

"Everything is fine. It's just that your mother and I will be celebrating our fiftieth wedding anniversary soon."

"Oh." He was right, their anniversary fell right around Thanksgiving. "I'm so grateful you still have each other."

"I wanted to do something special for her. Really make a big deal out of it. Fifty years is a long time, you know."

"It sure is," Janet said. "I think that's a great idea. What do you have in mind?"

"Well, at first I thought of taking her on a surprise vacation somewhere. She's always wanted to see Ireland. But then I remembered your mother hates planes, and it's such a long flight to get there."

"I don't know. I think it might be worth it. She'd love it."

"Yes, well, I did some research into the price of flights, and I thought it might be better to do something else. Even cruises are out of my range." Janet stifled a laugh. Her dad was a retired CPA and notoriously thrifty. She was not at all surprised to know that he didn't want to part with the money it would cost to take her mom to Europe. And Janet couldn't exactly blame him—traveling *was* expensive.

"What else are you thinking?"

"Well, I thought a party might be nice. Not a big gathering, just some of our friends, people from church, that kind of thing."

"That sounds nice. I bet Mom would love that."

"I'm glad you agree. The thing is... Well, I was hoping to make it a surprise. Which means I can't really do it at the house, you see."

Janet understood where this was headed now. "Did you want to have it here, at the café?"

"I was thinking that might be nice." He coughed. "And it would be cheaper than renting out the fellowship hall at the church."

There it was. She didn't stifle the laugh this time. They hadn't hosted parties, though she supposed they could. They'd had an after-homecoming gathering at the café last month, and it had turned out well. They didn't have a lot of space, so it would depend on how many people he'd be inviting.

"How big a crowd are you planning?" she asked.

"I'd say somewhere between thirty and forty," he said. "I think that's a good size for a party."

They could accommodate that number. They'd have to bring in a few more chairs, but it was doable.

"When were you thinking?" The café wouldn't be ready to host anything this week.

"A week from Saturday?"

That would make it the Saturday before Thanksgiving. She thought the café should be ready by that time, if Jaxon repainted the walls today and Greg had that glass for the door on order. She didn't have anything else going on that night. Maybe Tiffany would even come home from college early for the holiday. "Hang on. Let me ask Debbie about it."

She put her hand over the phone and turned to Debbie. "My dad is asking if he can use the café for a surprise anniversary party for my mom a week from Saturday."

"Aw, that's so nice." Debbie set down the frame she was working on and straightened up. "I don't see why not. That sounds like fun."

"Thanks. I'll let him know." She put the phone back to her ear. "That's fine, Dad. We'll need to talk about the menu and everything, but for now, let's plan on that."

"That's great news," Dad said. "Thank you."

"Of course."

"Just remember, Janet, it's a secret, so don't tell your mother."

"I won't, Dad."

After she hung up, they continued cleaning the frames, and it wasn't long before they had them all sparkling once again.

"We can leave these to dry and get them back on the walls after Jaxon paints," Debbie said.

"That sounds good." Janet straightened up and stretched. "I was thinking I might go over to see Kim and ask her about getting another print of that missing photo."

"I'll come with you." Debbie looked around the empty café. Most of their regulars had already come by, and they'd called Paulette to tell her not to bother coming in. "I think we've sold about as much coffee as we're going to today."

They turned out the lights and walked over to the museum, where there was a busload of children marveling over the model train display in one of the galleries. Probably a local elementary school class on a field trip.

"Good morning," Kim said when they entered her office. A small window let her see people standing at the front counter. "Are you all okay? I heard about the excitement over at the café this morning."

"We're doing all right," Debbie said.

Kim Smith was the curator of the Dennison Depot Museum, and Janet and Debbie had worked with her many times since opening the café. Her short hair was brushed back behind her ears, and she wore a neat navy blazer over her red turtleneck. There was music playing in the background—Janet recognized the voice of Nat King Cole. "How are you both doing? What a way to start the day, right?" Kim gestured for them to sit in the chairs across from her desk.

"It could have been a lot worse." Janet thought again how she was glad to live in a place where neighbors cared about one another, but she was already starting to get weary of retelling the story.

"I saw the police car when I drove up this morning, and I was so worried. What a terrible thing, and right after that great publicity too," Kim said. "Ian came over and asked for a copy of the museum's security camera footage from last night, so hopefully that will turn up some leads. But he says they didn't get anything of value, whoever it was."

"The only thing the thief took was one of the historic photos," Debbie said. "It's only valuable for sentimental reasons."

"What?" Kim's mouth dropped open. "Why would someone take an old photo of the depot?"

"We don't know." Janet shrugged. "We suspect probably out of spite when they couldn't get the cash register open, but of course we can't say for sure."

"Most likely it was a break-in gone wrong," Debbie added. "It seems like the thief did whatever he could to make a mess when he saw he couldn't get the money." She frowned. "Although, come to think of it, they brought the spray paint with them, so I guess they planned to make a mess whether they got any cash or not."

"I'm so sorry. That's awful." Kim sat up straighter in her chair. "And after you chose those photos so carefully too. Which one did they take?"

"It was the one of three young women standing behind a table in front of the depot," Janet said. "There's a briefcase on the table."

Kim narrowed her eyes. "I think I remember it. The Armistice Day photo? Were the women wearing poppies?"

"I don't know." Janet tried to picture the photograph again. "Maybe? I think they might have been wearing flowers of some kind."

"I bet that's it." Kim pushed herself up. "Come on. Let's go see if we can find the original in the archive, and we'll get you another copy."

They followed after her, and as they walked, Janet thought about Armistice Day. "Armistice Day was the precursor to Veterans Day, right?"

"That's right," Kim said as she started up the stairs. "It's celebrated on November 11, since the armistice that ended the fighting was signed on the eleventh hour of the eleventh day of the eleventh month in 1918."

"But what do poppies have to do with anything?" Janet held on to the handrail and made her way up the wooden stairs. "How do they symbolize fallen soldiers?"

"It came from the poem, 'In Flanders Fields,' written by a Canadian physician named John McCrae in 1915. It's about a dismal World War I battlefield where even in death, beauty grows. The poppy is a traditional symbol of death and rest, and the poem is a plea for those who come after to carry on the fight. The poem was so popular that people started wearing poppies as a symbol of Armistice Day."

Kim pushed the back-room door open, and they all stepped inside a large open area with filing cabinets along one wall. Shelves stacked with books and binders lined another wall. A large table in the middle of the room stood empty, as did the research computer terminals. Big windows let in the bright autumn sunshine. Kim walked over to one of the binders and began paging through the plastic-clad pages.

"Here we go." She carried the binder over to the table and opened it to the original black-and-white photo encased in a plastic sleeve. The picture showed the three women standing behind a table with the briefcase on top. Sure enough, now that Janet saw it again, she noticed that the women wore poppies pinned to their lapels.

"So the fact that the women in our photo wore poppies means the photo was taken on November 11?" Debbie asked.

"Almost certainly." Kim nodded. "Though what year, I don't know."

"Huh. I had no idea," Janet said. "But now that I know what day they were commemorating, I love the picture even more."

Kim turned the page and looked at the back of the photo to see if anything was written on it but shook her head when she saw it was blank. "Well, it was taken some time in the early forties, obviously."

She shrugged and flipped the page so they could see the photograph again. "Actually…"

Janet waited for her to go on, but Kim bit her lip, looking down at the photo.

"What is it?" Debbie asked.

"Oh my goodness. The briefcase! I don't know how I didn't put it together right away."

"Put what together?" Janet asked.

"This was *that* day."

"What day?" Why was Kim being so cryptic?

"Hang on." Kim set the binder on the table and walked over to one of the filing cabinets. She opened the second drawer and started rummaging through it. Janet looked at Debbie, who shrugged. Kim muttered to herself as she sorted through the files in the drawer. "Aha," she finally said. She pulled out a file folder and carried it over to the table. "Here we go."

Janet looked down and saw a copy of the *Evening Chronicle*, the local paper that was published in the area until 1981. Hospital Money Stolen from Donation Event, read the headline at the top of the page. The paper had been published on November 13, 1944.

"I can't believe I didn't put two and two together before," Kim said. "I was so excited about the poppies that I didn't pay attention to the briefcase. But it must be the briefcase that went missing."

"Wait. What happened?" Janet asked. She leaned forward and squinted at the small type on the yellowed page.

"This was a big deal," Kim said. "A wealthy man in town named Wilbur Finnegan decided to make a donation to the local hospital."

"Ten thousand dollars," Debbie said, reading from the article. "That was a lot of money in those days."

"It's a lot of money today," Janet said.

"It was a huge amount back then," Kim agreed. "The money was supposed to be to help treat the wounded soldiers who came through town. Because it was so much money, there was a lot of pomp and circumstance around the donation. There was supposed to be a whole ceremony where Finnegan handed the money over to the head of the hospital."

"Like, he was going to hand him ten thousand dollars in cash?" Janet asked.

"This was before electronic transfers," Kim said with a laugh. "I suppose these days they'd probably use an oversized cardboard check for the photo op, but Wilbur brought the actual cash to donate."

"That's a lot of bills," Janet said.

"But before the ceremony started, the briefcase containing the money went missing," Debbie said, looking up from the newspaper.

"How does a briefcase with ten thousand dollars in it go missing from the ceremony where it's supposed to be donated?" Janet asked.

Kim shrugged. "As far as I know, the briefcase was never found and the cash was never recovered."

"And this picture was taken that day?" Janet peered down at the photograph again.

"I think it must have been," Kim said. "And it shows the briefcase, so the photo was clearly taken before the briefcase went missing."

"It's almost eerie," Janet said. "It's like seeing a crime scene moments before the crime occurs."

"It's not *like* that, it *is* that," Kim said.

They were all quiet for a moment, thinking this through. Janet used her phone to take a picture of the article and accompanying photograph.

"To think of all that cash sitting inside that briefcase," Debbie said, shaking her head. "And then, boom, it vanishes, just like that."

Janet couldn't believe it. It seemed so bizarre that they had unknowingly picked out a photograph that showed the day of the theft at all, let alone one with the briefcase in the shot. She had simply liked the picture and thought it was an interesting glimpse into the history of the depot. Clearly there was more going on in the photo than she'd realized.

"What did Armistice Day have to do with the donation?" Janet asked. "Was it scheduled for that day on purpose?"

"I imagine it could have been a coincidence, but I don't know," Kim said.

"Did the police ever find any leads about what happened to the money?" Debbie asked.

"I know they looked into it thoroughly, but I don't think they ever got answers," Kim said. "Mom once told me about it and what a big deal the theft was. I don't think she ever forgave herself for letting it happen on her watch."

Kim's mother, Eileen, had been the stationmaster during the war after her predecessor was called into active military duty.

"I wonder what it means that this picture was the only thing stolen from the café," Janet said, shaking her head. "It's so random." Did the other pictures on their walls also have hidden backstories they hadn't yet uncovered?

"But what if it wasn't random?" Debbie asked.

"What?" Janet stared at her.

"What if it wasn't random that this photo was the only thing taken from the café?"

Janet blinked, trying to understand. "You mean, what if someone broke in just to take that picture?"

"I'm not saying it happened, I'm only asking what if," Debbie said. "What if there's a reason that particular picture was taken?"

"Why would someone break in to steal a picture?" Janet asked.

"You're saying, what if someone knew what this photo showed," Kim said.

Debbie nodded, and Janet started to understand what she was really saying.

"You think someone saw the photo hanging on the wall of the café and knew what that briefcase was and what this photo represented, and that's why they took it?" she asked.

"I'm just saying it's possible," Debbie said. "What if someone understood that this photo contained a clue about what really happened to the money that day? And that someone saw the photo hanging on our wall, recognized it for what it was, and decided to make it go away before anyone else figured out what it represented."

"It seems unlikely," Kim said dubiously. "The attempt to get into the cash register makes more sense, don't you think?"

"Maybe they tried to open the cash register but then saw the photo and went for it instead," Janet said. "Stealing money does make more sense, but I don't think we should dismiss the possibility of what Debbie is suggesting."

Debbie looked like she was going to say more, but didn't.

"What is it?" Janet asked.

"I was just thinking it might help if we could find out more about what happened the day the briefcase went missing." Debbie focused on Kim. "You said your mom was here that day. Do you think she'd be willing to talk to us about it?"

Eileen lived in a local retirement center, and her mind was still sharp. She often remembered events long in the past with great detail.

"I'm sure she would be happy to talk to you about it," Kim said.

"It can't hurt to talk to her," Debbie said. "It probably won't help us figure out who broke into the café, but we might learn more about what was going on in that photo and why someone might want to take it."

"And it never hurt anyone to learn a little bit more about history," Janet said with a smile.

CHAPTER THREE

*J*anet took a photo of the picture with her phone. She would come back later to take the original to the photo shop so they could have another copy made. For now, they got in the car and drove to Good Shepherd Retirement Home, which sat on the outskirts of town and was surrounded by rolling green grass and pine trees. They parked in the small lot and walked inside.

"Hello, Debbie," said Mary Knight from behind the front desk. Mary had been one of the daytime receptionists at the center for years, and since Debbie's father once managed the facility, Debbie knew her well.

"Hi, Mary. How are you today?"

"Just fine, thanks."

"You remember my friend Janet Shaw?"

"I do. It's nice to see you again." Mary's round face was surrounded by curly brown hair, and her scrubs had cartoon turkeys on them.

Janet smiled. "It's nice to see you again too."

"We're here to see Eileen Palmer," Debbie said. "Do you happen to know where she is?"

"Last time I saw her, she was in the library doing a puzzle," Mary said. "I'd check there."

"Thank you." After the two of them signed in, they went past a large sitting area, where some residents were gathered in groups at tables chatting or watching television at the front of the room. The library was halfway down the hallway on the left side, and they stepped in to find several residents gathered around a card table, working on a jigsaw puzzle of fall foliage surrounding a charming English cottage. A woman with frizzy white hair sat across from Eileen, picking pieces out of the box. The walls of the room were lined with shelves stuffed with books of all kinds, and a stack of board games sat on a table to one side.

"Well, hello there," Eileen said. "Looks like we have some visitors."

"Hi, Eileen," Janet said. "It's good to see you."

"It's good to see both of you," Eileen said. She turned to her friend. "This is Bridie." She raised her voice. "Bridie, this is Janet and Debbie. They're the ones who run the Whistle Stop Café—you know, it used to be the old railroad canteen."

Bridie nodded and smiled but didn't respond.

"We were hoping to talk to you if you have some time," Debbie said.

"Oh, I've got nothing but time." Eileen slowly pushed herself up. Janet resisted the urge to rush forward and help her. Eileen could still get around on her own, and Janet knew it was important to let her.

"Let's go to my room," she said. Then she turned to Bridie and raised her voice again. "We're going to go to my room. I'll come back when we're done talking."

Again, Bridie smiled but didn't say anything. Eileen led them out of the library and into the hallway.

"She doesn't say much, but that's why I like her," Eileen said once they were in the hallway. "Some of the people around here never stop talking. It's nice to just sit in peace sometimes."

Janet stifled a laugh and followed Eileen. At the end of the hall, they turned into a room that had EILEEN TURNER PALMER engraved on the nameplate beneath a photo of Eileen in her stationmaster outfit, shoulder-length blond hair flowing out behind her as she stood in the open doorway of a train. She led them inside her room, which had a twin bed in one corner and a seating area in the other, near a window that looked out over a grove of trees.

"Now, then." She settled into a well-worn recliner and gestured for them to take a seat in the wingback chairs. "What brings you to see me today?"

"We're interested in finding out about a theft that happened at the station back in November 1944." Janet sat down in one of the chairs, which was upholstered in an itchy crewelwork fabric. "We understand a briefcase full of money was stolen just before it was to be donated to the hospital."

"Oh yes." Eileen nodded. "I remember, all right. That was a terrible day."

"We believe this picture was taken that day," Janet said. She swiped to the photo and held her phone out so Eileen could see it. Eileen leaned forward.

"Would you look at that?" Eileen let out a long breath. "That was it, all right. And the briefcase is right there in the picture. This was taken before it was stolen, then."

"That's what we understand," Janet said.

"Wow." She let out a long breath. "That brings back so many memories." She paused again. "What a strange day."

"Can you tell us what you remember?" Debbie asked.

"Well, it was a big deal, you see. Wilbur Finnegan was making a huge donation to the hospital. He was a big man in town then—president of the bank, head of the Dennison Chamber of Commerce, on the town board. He had a lot of power back then, and here he was, making such a generous donation to the war effort. Mayor Humphreys decided to make a ceremony out of it. There were going to be speeches, Mason Jenson from the hospital was supposed to talk about how the money would allow them to build a new wing to care for the wounded, and there was supposed to be a big moment where Finnegan handed over the briefcase. The band from the high school was going to play 'The 1812 Overture' and 'The Stars and Stripes Forever' at the end of the ceremony. We were all beside ourselves, trying to make sure the whole thing went off without a hitch."

"Why did they choose the depot as the location for the ceremony?" Janet asked.

"I suppose because it had the most direct tie to the war effort," Eileen said. "Because of how the canteen gave away meals to the soldiers passing through every day. It was such a symbol of what the people in this town and the surrounding area were doing to help the men and women in uniform, so it seemed like the best place for it. At least, that's what I assumed. I wasn't exactly asked if the ceremony could be hosted at the station, mind you. Mayor Humphreys said this was where it would be, and so it was."

"Were you okay with that?" Janet asked.

"Oh, yes. We were all very excited about the whole thing," Eileen said. "They scheduled it for Armistice Day, supposedly to give it even more meaning, though I think the timing was just convenient, personally. And like I said, we worked hard to make sure everything went smoothly, though, as you know, it didn't exactly go as planned."

"Can you tell us what happened?" Janet asked.

Eileen adjusted a pillow against her lower back. "Well, Wilbur brought the briefcase just as he'd promised. He showed it to Mayor Humphreys and Mr. Jenson. From what I understand, he even opened it up to show them that the cash was inside, though I didn't see that myself."

"So there was proof that the cash was actually inside the briefcase," Debbie said.

"Indeed," Eileen said with a wry grin. "Then Wilbur carried it over to the table we'd set up. There was supposed to be a photo shoot for the paper, or posterity, or I don't know what. And I don't know who decided which of the canteen girls was going to be in the shots, but it ended up being Jean, Gayle, and Dorinda."

"Gayle?" Janet asked. Gayle was Ray Zink's younger sister's name, and she was still full of life in her nineties. Gayle had recently come to Dennison for a visit. Ray was a World War II veteran and a fixture in town. He had owned the house Debbie bought when she moved back to Dennison, but now Ray lived at Good Shepherd. "Do you mean Gayle Bailey?"

"I do," Eileen said, smiling.

Janet leaned forward and squinted. It did look like a younger version of her, now that Eileen pointed it out.

"You should talk to her," Eileen said. "She may be able to tell you more."

"We will," Debbie said. "How about the others? Are they still around?"

"No, I don't think so. Jean passed away many years ago. I didn't really keep up with Dorinda after she left the area, but I suspect chances are slim."

"So Gayle was there when the briefcase went missing?" Debbie asked.

"She was. All of them were, and so was Wilbur. But those girls all said they didn't see what happened to it."

"How is that possible though?" Janet didn't understand. "One minute it was there on the table, the next it was gone, and none of the people who were nearby saw the briefcase disappear? How can that be?"

"Well now, a couple of things happened that might explain it," Eileen said. "The first is named Jamison Finnegan, and the second is Jasper Finnegan."

"Who were they?" Janet asked.

"Wilbur's sons. They worked with him at the bank and were considered to be the most eligible bachelors in town." She sniffed. "Of course, it could have had something to do with the fact that they were the only bachelors in town at that point."

"I imagine single men were hard to come by," Debbie said. "They didn't join up?"

"They tried, but some kind of medical issue prevented them. I think they both had a heart condition. Anyway, the two of them were on hand that day, and I saw both of them flirting with those girls after the photo shoot."

"Jasper and Jamison were near the table where the briefcase was?" Janet asked.

"Not near it, exactly," Eileen said. "From what I saw, the girls stepped away from the table to talk to the boys."

"They didn't keep their eyes on the briefcase?" Debbie asked.

"I suppose they thought their job was done. They weren't there as security guards," Eileen said. "They were just there to make a pretty picture. And Wilbur was right there, keeping an eye on it. He was intent on not letting it out of his sight."

"But he must have looked away too," Debbie said. "How did that happen?"

"Well, that was the fault of the cannon."

"The cannon?" Janet couldn't have heard that right.

"Like I said, the high school band was there to play a couple of songs. 'The Stars and Stripes Forever' and the '1812 Overture.' You've heard them?"

"Of course," Janet said. "My mom loves to watch the Boston Pops Fourth of July celebration on TV. Every year they play 'The Stars and Stripes Forever' and end with 'The 1812 Overture.' She loves to watch the fireworks explode over the Charles River as those are played."

"I enjoy that broadcast too," Debbie said. "Though I'll never understand why 'The 1812 Overture' is seen as a patriotic song, considering it was written by Tchaikovsky to celebrate Russia's defense against Napoleon's armies."

"It's a wonderful piece though," Eileen said. "The high school band practiced it for weeks, and the kids were excited to perform it. There was just one problem."

"The cannon," Janet said.

"That's right." Eileen nodded. "If you've heard 'The 1812 Overture,' you know the climactic movement involves a volley of cannon fire."

"Most orchestras use recorded cannon fire these days," Debbie said. "But you're saying they had an actual cannon?"

"It turns out the band director was a World War I fanatic, and he had a whole collection of weapons from the war in his collection, including a cannon."

"He brought his own cannon to the celebration?" Janet asked. It was so ridiculous it was almost funny.

"Like I said, this ceremony was a big deal," Eileen said. "There was a lot of discussion about this cannon ahead of time, believe you me. I wasn't sure it would be safe to have it at the depot with so many people around. But he assured all of us that they weren't firing actual cannonballs or anything like that. They were just blanks, and he would be in charge of the cannon himself, and it would all be perfectly safe. In the end we decided to let him go ahead with it."

"But I thought you said the band wasn't supposed to play until after the ceremony," Debbie said.

"It wasn't. They didn't." Eileen adjusted in her chair. "But as they were getting the cannon set up before the ceremony started, it went off somehow."

"How does a cannon accidentally fire?" Janet couldn't understand it. "It's not like a gun where you load a round of bullets, is it? Don't you have to load each shot individually?" She tried to recall the videos she'd seen of the Boston Pops. Didn't they have members of the military load the shots one at a time? And those were modern cannons, not from World War I.

"I don't know how it happened," Eileen said. "I'm not sure we ever got a good answer on that. All I know is that it went off and scared the living daylights out of everyone at the depot."

"I can imagine." Janet couldn't think of too many things more startling than the boom of a cannon when you weren't expecting it.

"No one was hurt, thankfully. Again, the band director insisted nobody had ever been in danger, as they were not firing real shots, but that didn't make anyone feel any better."

"So the cannon went off, and that was enough to distract everyone," Debbie said.

"That's right," Eileen said. "Including Wilbur Finnegan. Come to find out, he was a veteran, and the sound brought back memories of his time in the trenches. He went into... Well, I suppose you'd call it a panic attack these days. PTSD or something. We called it shell shock in my day. Dr. Ellington had to administer a sedative to calm him down."

"How awful," Janet said.

"It was really sad," Eileen said. "And naturally, the girls and Wilbur's sons concentrated on helping him, not guarding the briefcase. And, well, by the time everything calmed down, the briefcase was gone. No one could say what happened to it. Everyone insisted they hadn't seen a thing."

Janet tried to imagine it. The boom of the cannon amid the casual chatter. Every head would have turned toward the sound. Everyone would have been focused on figuring out what had caused it. It would have been reason enough for Wilbur Finnegan to have taken his eyes off the briefcase, especially if the sound thrust him back into the trenches of World War I. It wouldn't have taken long for someone to snatch the briefcase while everyone was distracted. It could have happened in the blink of an eye.

"No one would even look twice at someone walking around with a briefcase at a train station," Debbie said, shaking her head.

"But it would have to be someone who was physically near the table when the cannon went off," Janet said.

"That was the theory," Eileen said. "But there weren't very many people it could have been—just the three canteen girls and Wilbur."

"What about Jamison and Jasper?"

"They were on the far side of the girls. They would have to go past the women to get to the table, and all of them said that didn't happen."

"So there were only four suspects?"

Eileen nodded. "All three of the women insisted they had nothing to do with it. Wilbur couldn't have done it, not the way he reacted to that cannon. He wasn't thinking about the money or anything else in that moment. I felt so bad for him."

"But someone had to have seen something," Debbie insisted. "It didn't just vanish."

Eileen shrugged. "If they did, they didn't come forward."

"Someone wasn't telling the truth," Janet said. "Someone knows what happened to that briefcase."

"Someone undoubtedly did," Eileen said. "And if this happened today, I'm sure the whole thing would have been caught on security cameras and a dozen cell phones. But none of that existed back then. They looked at all the photos they had of the event, and they didn't find any clues. The police were never able to find anyone who could say how it transpired."

"The money was never recovered, from what we understand," Debbie said.

"That's true," Eileen confirmed.

But someone knew something. A thief had taken the money, and it seemed likely that someone living today knew the answers, Janet was growing more certain. And if she was right, that someone had taken the picture from the wall of their café in hopes that no one else figured out where the money had gone.

CHAPTER FOUR

*J*anet and Debbie stopped by Ray Zink's room before they left Good Shepherd, but he was asleep in his wheelchair, and they didn't want to disturb him. They would try talking to him some other time. Debbie was quiet when they got back in the car. Janet waited for her to start the vehicle, but she didn't.

"What's wrong?" Janet asked.

"Nothing, really," Debbie said. "I was just thinking."

"Well, don't let me stop you."

Debbie gave her a wry smile. "I was thinking how we could be on a wild goose chase and whoever broke in just wanted to rob the place."

"Right," Janet said. "I'm sure that's the angle the police are working on."

Debbie started the car. "I wonder if they have any leads or suspects about who it could be, if that's the case."

"Well..." Janet thought for a moment. What was that bit that Ian and Deputy Vaughn hadn't wanted her to overhear? "I heard Ian saying something about an auto parts store."

"An auto parts store?" Debbie wrinkled her nose. "What did they say?"

"It wasn't very clear, but I got the impression it had something to do with a robbery at one recently." She thought back, trying to make sense of it. "And they said something about how the person who broke in just got out."

"Of jail?"

"That's what I assumed."

"Did they say who it was?"

Janet closed her eyes and tried to remember. Hadn't Ian said a name? Smaller? Smolder? Smeed? "I'm sorry. They did, but I don't remember what it was."

"But you're saying it sounds like they're thinking that maybe the person who broke into the auto parts store got out of jail and is up to their old tricks?"

"That's what it sounded like," Janet said. "I'm sorry I can't tell you more. They acted like they didn't want me to hear what they were saying."

"Good for you for listening anyway." Debbie grinned. "Okay, so one potential lead is that it's the same person who broke into the auto parts store. We might be able to learn more about who that was. But there's also the other reason someone might have broken in."

"The Alyssa theory," Janet said. "There's the possibility that she—or someone she knows—broke in just to wreak havoc on the café, out of jealousy."

"Or greed," Debbie said. "She's trying to get a small business off the ground. Never underestimate the lure of greed."

Janet nodded. "Do you really think she would do something like that though?"

"She was the first person we both thought of when they asked us for ideas," Debbie said.

"I guess that's true."

"It's not only the strange things she's said to us," Debbie said. "There's just something off about her. She's too eager, too earnest somehow."

Janet wanted to laugh. "I've never heard 'eager' and 'earnest' used as bad characteristics before."

"You know what I mean. It's like she thinks for her business to succeed, ours has to fail."

"Right." It was true, Alyssa did give off that impression. "Well, I'm sure Ian spoke to her. If she had anything to do with it, he'll know."

"You're right," Debbie said.

"What?"

"What do you mean, what?"

"You're not satisfied with that, are you?"

"It's not that." Debbie let out a sigh. "It's not that I don't think Ian will figure out if she's guilty. Ian and his team are top-notch. It's just that I can't help wondering what Alyssa would say if we talked to her. Like, how would she react if she saw us? Would she give anything away? Would we be able to tell if she had anything to do with it?"

"Ian probably wouldn't like it if we interfered with his investigation."

"We wouldn't interfere," Debbie said. "It would be more that we'd be seeing for ourselves what she has to say. It would be supplementing their work."

Janet glanced at the clock. There was still another hour until school let out and Jaxon would be heading to the café. "You know, I am craving doughnuts…"

"It won't mess with Ian's investigation for us to go to Glazed and look around," Debbie said with a smile.

"And if we happen to run into Alyssa there, it would be rude not to talk to her," Janet said.

"All right then," Debbie said, putting the car into gear. "It looks like a side trip to Uhrichsville is in order."

The small towns of Dennison and Uhrichsville sat right next to each other, on opposite sides of Stillwater Creek. Janet and Debbie crossed the small bridge and made their way to the quaint downtown area of Uhrichsville, where the streets were lined with old brick buildings. Debbie pulled into a parking spot in front of the space where Third Street Bakery had been. Now, the plate-glass window that faced the street had the word GLAZED printed in a modern-looking font. Through the window, Janet could see that the once cheerful pink walls were now painted a charcoal gray, and the display case had been replaced by a long wooden bar fronted with glass. Behind the register, the day's flavors were written on a chalkboard, and a selection of T-shirts and sweatshirts with the store's logo hung along the wall, available for purchase.

"Well, this looks different," Debbie said. Janet was busy trying to take it in. She'd known that Alyssa would change the space—of course she'd want to make it her own. But she was still surprised at how much it affected her to see the place where she'd spent so many years of her life baking turned into something so completely different. Only the high tin ceilings and the light oak floors remained the same.

They stepped inside and Janet saw that, behind the glass, there were dozens of doughnuts piled along the bar. The sugary icing glistened under the pendant lights. She read the list of doughnut flavors available that day—rosewater and vanilla, chai, sriracha, maple and bacon, s'mores… They sounded bizarre, but Janet had to admit they looked pretty good.

She was still trying to figure out what she was going to say when suddenly Alyssa stepped out from the back.

"Hello." Alyssa smiled as she came toward them. Her red hair hung down her back, and she wore jeans and an oversized sweatshirt. A nose ring flashed as she moved. "Janet, Debbie. How are you two doing? I heard about what happened at the café, and I am so sorry."

"Thank you," Debbie said, stepping forward. "It's such a shock."

"I can't even imagine." Alyssa shook her head. "I was thinking just before you came in how random it was. Who would break into your sweet little café?"

"We wish we knew," Debbie said.

"I heard that you discovered it when you got there this morning," Alyssa said to Janet. "That must have been so scary. Do they know when it happened?"

"Sometime last night," Janet said. "I don't know if they know what time yet."

"Ugh. It's just so creepy," Alyssa said. "To think, while I was sleeping safe and sound at my mom's house, this horrible thing was happening."

"You slept at your mom's house?" Janet cocked her head. She didn't know much about Alyssa's personal life, but she'd heard that the owner of Glazed lived in the apartment over the donut shop.

"Oh, yeah. That's not, like, a normal thing or anything. I have my own apartment. But my mom had surgery on Friday, so I'm staying with her until she's back on her feet."

"That's nice of you." Janet felt a pang of sadness. Tiffany had started college this fall, and Janet missed her terribly. It was nice to hear that Alyssa prioritized her family.

"I mean, it's just the two of us, you know? My dad left when I was young, and Mom has worked so hard for so long to provide for us. It's nice to be able to help her out for a change."

"I imagine you must be under a lot of pressure to make this business work, in that case," Debbie said. "It's a big deal for someone as young as you to own her own business."

"I do feel pressure," Alyssa said, nodding. "But business is going really well. I mean, our doughnuts are really good, if I do say so myself. Have you tried them?"

"Not yet," Janet admitted. She supposed they should, now that they were here.

"Here, please, have a doughnut, on the house. My pathetic way of saying I'm sorry about what happened."

"Oh." Janet shook her head. "That's not necessary."

"I know that, but I insist. Come on." She gestured at the selection laid out on the counter. "What kind do you want?"

Janet bit her lip. She wasn't one to turn down a free doughnut, and they did look good. She scanned the flavor options, hoping for something that sounded, well, normal.

"I'd love to try the toasted coconut," Debbie said.

Janet wasn't a huge fan of coconut. "Do you have anything like a plain chocolate?"

"You should have the salted Nutella one," Alyssa said. "That's chocolate and hazelnut with sea salt, and it's one of my favorites."

A salty doughnut? That didn't sound too bad.

Alyssa picked up the doughnuts with wax paper, set them inside little white bags, and handed them over the glass partition. "Enjoy." Somewhere in the back, a phone rang. "Sorry, I've got to get that, but thank you for stopping by."

She waved and disappeared through the door. Janet looked at Debbie, who shrugged and led her out of the shop. Janet pulled her coat tighter around herself, bracing against the bitter wind, and when they got back inside the car, Debbie turned on the engine.

"What did you think?" Debbie asked, and then took a bite of her doughnut. "Oh, wow. This is good."

"I thought she was… Well, she was actually kind of sweet," Janet said. "I thought it was nice that she's taking care of her mom, and it was nice of her to give us doughnuts."

"Try yours," Debbie said, and then took another bite of hers. The air coming out of the vents started to warm.

Janet slid the doughnut out of its bag and took a bite. Debbie was right. It was delicious. Cakey and gooey, and the chocolate and hazelnut flavors were fantastic. The salt didn't make it weird at all. "This is a good doughnut."

"This is a *fantastic* doughnut." Debbie took another bite of hers. "So, you believed her?"

"Believed her? About what?"

"I don't know. The whole act."

"I guess I did. You didn't?"

"No way. Not at all."

Janet turned in her seat. "How come?"

Debbie held up a finger and polished off her doughnut. While she chewed, she brushed toasted coconut flakes off her fingers and into the wax bag. Janet ate more of her doughnut. How did Alyssa get them this fluffy? And this moist without being greasy?

"First off," Debbie said after she swallowed, "she was like a totally different person. Every time she's come into our shop, she's had this weird competitive thing going on. She's never just been, well, nice."

"You don't think she was being nice because she felt bad for us?"

"I could buy that, except for the other things."

"What other things?"

"For one, she never asked what we were doing there. It was like she expected us."

"I guess that's true." Janet played the interaction back in her head. "But why would she be expecting us?"

"Maybe because she knows she's a suspect," Debbie said. "Because the police have already been there to talk with her, right?"

Ian had said they were going to talk to her this morning. Janet nodded.

"She knew about the break-in and how you discovered it this morning, but she didn't mention the fact that the police had been in to question her."

"There could be lots of reasons she might not have mentioned that," Janet said. "It's not exactly good for business to have the police show up."

"I still think it's noticeably odd to leave something like that out," Debbie said. "But then there's the fact that she gave herself an alibi without our asking her about where she was."

She had done that, Janet realized. "You're right. She was pretty quick to volunteer the fact that she was with her mom last night, even though no one asked."

"She didn't hesitate. And it was a nice, wholesome alibi that would make us feel warm and fuzzy toward her. It totally worked on you." Debbie gave her a knowing look.

"It…" Okay, it had worked on her. "Fine. But that doesn't mean it's not true."

"It may very well be true that she was with her mom. But even if she was, she could have slipped away, right? If her mom just had surgery, she's probably on painkillers. She may not have noticed if Alyssa slipped away in the middle of the night. The alibi isn't actually all that solid, but that's not my point. I'm simply commenting on the fact that she absolutely made sure to give us an alibi, with no prompting from us. Don't you think that's weird?"

"Okay," Janet said. "I see what you're saying. But it's no weirder than her telling us she wants us out of business."

"True enough. But there is one other thing that puts her squarely in the category of prime suspect."

"What's that?"

"Did you notice that bandage on her wrist?"

"What?" Janet shook her head. "No."

"I saw it when her sleeve pulled up when she reached for the doughnuts. She has a decent-sized patch of gauze and medical tape on her wrist."

"I didn't notice it," Janet said. "You're thinking of the blood on the glass from the door."

"Precisely."

"It could have been caused by anything though. We don't know that it's related to our break-in."

"Of course we don't know. But as soon as she saw me notice it, she ran off."

"The phone was ringing."

"Well, that's true. But still, there's enough there to make me think she could be the one."

Debbie was right. Taken together, all those little things did add up to a strange encounter, and one that didn't make Alyssa seem as innocent as Janet had first thought.

"How did I miss all that?" Janet asked.

"You're trusting," Debbie said. "You always see the good in people. And that's not a bad thing."

"But I clearly didn't pick up on any of that."

"That's why we make a good team."

Janet couldn't disagree. "Okay, let's say she was behind the break-in. What would she want with the picture of the briefcase?"

"Maybe nothing. It could have been what we first thought, that the picture was just a last-minute grab. An effort to cause more confusion. Alyssa's goal, if she is guilty, would have been to get our café to close for a while and drive our customers to her, in the hopes that they would become regulars."

"But no one was in her shop, so it didn't work."

Debbie shrugged. "It's also Tuesday afternoon. Not prime doughnut-buying time. Maybe some of our customers did come by this morning. Or maybe they didn't. In any case, I think she's suspicious enough that I'm putting her at the top of our suspect list."

"Technically, she's the only person on our suspect list," Janet said.

"Well, yes. And unless someone else is added, I think we work under the assumption she was behind the break-in."

"Huh." Janet thought it all through again. "What do you think we should do about it?"

"First off, you should probably tell Ian about this conversation, just to make sure what she told us lines up with what she told him."

Janet nodded. She could do that.

"Second, I think we should keep looking into Alyssa. I know the police are on it and Ian is great at what he does, but I also know I want the thief caught, and if we can find out more about what she was really up to last night, that would help."

"Okay." Janet could see the wisdom in all those points.

"And third, you should finish your doughnut, because whether she's guilty or not, that girl knows how to fry."

CHAPTER FIVE

By the time they got back to Dennison, it was almost time for Jaxon to come by and get started on repainting the walls of the café. As they pulled up to the depot, Janet said, "Do you mind if I go to the library and let you take care of Jaxon?"

"No problem," Debbie said. "Got a hot date with a book?"

"I was actually thinking I might do some more research into the theft of that money. I want to see if there were any other newspaper articles about it. The library has a database that has access to the newspaper archives."

"That's a good idea. Have fun."

"You're sure you don't need me?"

"I'm sure. We just need someone here to let him in."

"All right then," Janet said. "Let me know how it goes."

Debbie waved, and Janet made the short drive to the Dennison branch of the Claymont Public Library. As she walked up to the door of the brick building, she saw paper turkeys taped to the glass. She stepped inside and breathed in deeply, taking in the sweet scent of thousands and thousands of beautiful books. Libraries smelled like heaven.

Ellie Cartwright was at the circulation desk. Ellie was the head librarian, and she was a whiz at finding whatever information was needed. She knew where every book was shelved and how to plumb every database, and she had an especially deep knowledge of Ohio history.

"Hi there, Janet," Ellie said. "I heard about the break-in this morning. I'm so sorry."

"Thank you," Janet said. "Thankfully, not much was taken. It's mostly just repainting and repairing the door."

"That's good news," Ellie said. She peered up at Janet through her glasses. Ellie had been two years behind Janet and Debbie in school. Her long brown hair, streaked with just a hint of gray, was piled in a messy bun and held in place with two pens. Her daughter Catherine was a few years younger than Tiffany. "Is there anything I can do to help?"

"Not that I can think of," Janet said. "But thank you."

"Anytime. And hey, that was a great write-up in the *Plain Dealer*."

"Thank you. We were really happy about it." In all the excitement of the day, Janet had almost forgotten about the article. "I guess you win some and lose some, right?"

Ellie laughed. "Fair enough. Now, what can I help you find?"

"I was hoping to get into the genealogical database and the newspaper archives."

"Sure thing." Ellie stood and walked around the circulation desk. "Come this way."

Janet followed Ellie past a display of children's books about the first Thanksgiving and past the reading area toward the reference section, at the far end of the library. Ellie steered Janet to one of the computer terminals that lined the back wall.

"The databases are all available here," she said, clicking on an icon of a file folder. She navigated to an inner folder and then one more, and then she said, "Here you go. The newspaper databases are here. Are you looking for a local paper, or a national one?"

"Local," Janet said. "But from a long time ago."

"How long?"

"The 1940s."

"Then you probably want this one." Ellie clicked on a link, and a search page opened. "This is the archive of the *Evening Chronicle*, which was the main paper in this area until 1981. The *Times Reporter* is here."

Janet nodded, recognizing the name of the modern local paper, based in nearby New Philadelphia.

"And"—Ellie clicked back a few screens—"the genealogy program is here." She clicked on it, and a web browser opened. "It's one of those online sites that you normally pay for, but you get free access through the library."

"Thank you. I never would have found those on my own."

"Let me know if you need anything else." Ellie stood up and returned to the circulation desk, and Janet turned to the search screen. Since the genealogy site was open, she decided to start there. She assumed Wilbur Finnegan had passed some time ago, if he was a World War I veteran. But what about his sons, Jamison and Jasper? If Eileen was right, and they were near the briefcase on the day of the theft, they might have information about what really happened. Or, Janet couldn't help but think, one or both of them could have been responsible for it, even though Eileen said they couldn't be. In any case, if they were still around, they would be worth tracking down.

She typed the name *Wilbur Finnegan* into the search window and held her breath. So many people's family trees had been built out online, but it wasn't something she could count on. Still, several links popped up, and Janet clicked on the first one. It mentioned a Wilbur Finnegan who was born in County Cork, Ireland, in 1865. Was this Wilbur related to the Wilbur she was looking for? It was unclear, as this Wilbur appeared to be just a sidenote to the main branch of the family tree.

Janet clicked on the next link, and this one seemed like more of a possibility. This family tree had been created by a Maxine Walters, who was the granddaughter of a Wilbur Finnegan. This Wilbur Finnegan was born in 1898 in Chicago and married an Evelyn Pence in 1922. They had three children—three? Janet checked again and saw that she'd read that right. There was Jamison Finnegan, born in 1924, and Jasper Finnegan, born in 1925. Maxine Walters was Jasper's daughter, apparently. And next to Jasper's name, there was the name Norma Finnegan, the third child of Wilbur and Evelyn, born in 1939. Norma must have been something of a late-in-life surprise. She would have been just a child when the briefcase was stolen, which might explain why Eileen didn't mention her attendance at the event.

She looked back to the tree and saw that Jamison passed away in 1974 and Jasper had lived until 1999. So she wouldn't be able to talk to either of them. But their sister Norma was still alive, at least according to this family tree. She'd married a man named Leo Starr and had three children of her own. Did she live nearby? Would she know anything about the event? There was only one way to find out.

She clicked back to the main internet search page, typed in *Norma Starr*, and found her easily. She was on the board of an art museum in Columbus and listed as a deacon on the website of the First Episcopal Church. She was also the director of the Finnegan

Foundation, which was described as "a fund supporting the arts and culture." That was decidedly vague.

It seemed Norma was alive and lived in Columbus. That was about a two-hour drive, which would make talking to her in person tricky. She clicked on the contact information for the trust website and found the address. When she typed it in an online maps app, she discovered it was located about half an hour east of Columbus. That was more doable. She poked around on the site a bit more and found an email address for Norma. She typed up an email, asking Norma if she could ask some questions about her father, and hit send.

Next, she turned her attention to the newspaper archives, hoping she might find more articles about the theft. She narrowed the search window to November 11, 1944, through the end of that year, and she typed the search terms "briefcase" and "theft." She hit return and was pleased to see half a dozen results turn up. She clicked on the first link and found an image of the article dated November 13 that they'd seen earlier, just like the one that was in the museum's archives.

HOSPITAL MONEY STOLEN FROM DONATION EVENT

Police are stumped by the theft of a briefcase containing $10,000 in cash that was set to be donated to the Dennison Hospital yesterday. The briefcase vanished from outside the canteen at the Dennison train depot. The money, which was donated by local businessman Wilbur Finnegan, was to be handed over to Mayor Eric Humphreys at the conclusion of a short ceremony Saturday morning and was earmarked for a new trauma wing to treat returning servicemen.

Before the ceremony started, the briefcase was placed on a table outside the canteen, where photographs were to be taken for posterity. Humphreys said that the photo opportunity began around 9:45 a.m., with the donation ceremony set to begin at 10 a.m. Somehow, between the time the briefcase was photographed and the ceremony's start, it vanished.

Mayor Humphreys pleads for anyone with information concerning the whereabouts of the briefcase or its contents to please come forward.

There wasn't a lot of information there, at least nothing that Janet didn't already know. But this was printed two days after the theft. Maybe there had been an update once the press found time to interview the police and learn more. She clicked on the next link and discovered that it had been printed in the next edition, a week later, on November 20.

STILL NO LEADS IN BRIEFCASE THEFT

Police are asking for any information regarding the disappearance of a briefcase containing $10,000 in cash that disappeared from a table outside the Dennison train depot on Saturday, November 11. A few more details have emerged about what happened in the moments before the theft, but police are still looking for clues about the briefcase and its whereabouts.

The cash, donated by Wilbur Finnegan, of Finnegan Bank and Trust, was last seen on a table outside the depot, where it was displayed so photographs could be taken. One of the photographs taken in that shoot is printed alongside this article. Three women posed with the briefcase during the photo shoot—Jean Holcombe, Gayle Zink, and Dorinda Meyer—and all three have claimed innocence, though Police Chief William Bradley says that all three still remain persons of interest in the disappearance.

After the photo shoot, the women stood at the table near the briefcase, and Mayor Humphreys said that they were the only people near the briefcase aside from Mr. Finnegan, the donor.

Just moments before the briefcase was discovered missing, a loud boom was reported in the vicinity of the depot. Apparently a cannon, which was to be used by the high school band in their planned rendition of 'The 1812 Overture,' misfired, causing mayhem and distracting those near the table. It is believed that in the ensuing confusion, the briefcase was taken.

Anyone with any information about the missing briefcase is urged to get in contact with the police immediately.

Next to this article was the same photo that had been hanging in the café. The table was set apart from the station in an area clearly set up for the photo op. It wasn't so close to the station that people would have been coming and going all around it.

Where had the band been in relation to this table? Where was the cannon? She tried to imagine how it must have played out. The women, posing for photographs with the briefcase, an anxious Wilbur Finnegan hovering nearby. The unexpected boom of the cannon frightening the war veteran, bringing back memories of horror in the trenches. It must have been terrifying. Of course, they had all turned away from the briefcase, startled by the sudden noise and trying to find out where it came from.

But who was it who had swooped in during the ensuing chaos? Who was close enough to grab the case and devious or desperate enough to take it in the first place?

She sighed. This article didn't tell her much that she didn't already know, other than Dorinda's last name.

Janet read more follow-up articles, but none of them revealed any new information about the theft. The police didn't seem to uncover any leads or find any new possible suspects—at least none that were reported in the newspaper. How was that possible? And how was it possible that the money had never been recovered?

She extended the search parameters and looked for any additional articles about the theft, but aside from a follow-up at the one-year mark that reported nothing new had been found, she couldn't find anything else.

Janet sat back and stretched her arms overhead. Actually, while she was thinking about the break-in, there was one more thing she could research, since she was here. She knew Ian was looking into the theft and would find the culprit, but she couldn't stop thinking about it. It wouldn't hurt for her to do a little digging on her own, just to see what she found out. She wasn't going to do anything about it...

Ian had said something about the auto parts store and the name Smullen, or Smallen, or something like that. Those were close, anyway. She decided to start by seeing if she could find the guy with a simple internet search, but searching for *Smullen auto parts* and *Smallen auto parts* didn't get her anywhere. She'd have to try another way.

She clicked over to the database Ellie had shown her that searched the *Times Reporter*, the modern weekly newspaper in the area, and did a search for *Smallen* and then *Smullen*, but nothing came up. Maybe she could find it by searching for information about the auto parts store.

She didn't know if Deputy Vaughn had meant the one in the strip mall out by the highway or the one on the outskirts of Uhrichsville, but it shouldn't be that hard to figure out which one had been broken into. She typed in *auto parts* and *break-in*. Aha. There it was. Back in April, there was a short entry in a police blotter, which listed police activity from the week:

Police were called to Twin Cities Auto Parts and Repair on Monday morning to respond to a report of breaking and entering and theft. Authorities found the glass on the store's door smashed in and the scene in disarray, with parts reportedly pulled from shelves and thrown on the floor. The store's owner reports that nearly $2,000 was taken from the store's cash registers. Police are investigating the robbery and have asked for anyone who has information to come forward.

Well, it was clear why Ian and Deputy Vaughn had made the connection between the break-in that morning and the one at the auto parts store. It did seem to be similar enough that it could have been done by the same person. And they had mentioned that the thief was just out of prison. If only she could remember his name. She racked her brain, trying to recall it, but she couldn't bring it up.

Well, there had to be a way to find it. She thought for a moment and then decided to try a search for *Twin Cities Auto* in the archive. She hit return, and, right at the top, the first link that came up was one to an article titled SUSPECT ARRESTED IN TWIN CITIES ROBBERY. It was another short piece, but it did give the name of the man who was arrested for the break-in. Curtis Smollen. *Smollen!* She had been so close.

Now that she knew the name, it wouldn't be that hard to find out more about Curtis. She navigated to the main web browser and did a search for his name. She found him mentioned in a few social media posts, but they didn't seem to be the right Curtis. There was a profile of another Curtis Smollen on a web page for a hunting club. There was a picture accompanying the profile, and it showed a muscular man in his mid-to-late twenties with a shaggy brown beard and a baseball cap that said VALVOLINE. Was this him? The hunting club was in Uhrichsville, so it was certainly possible.

"Are you having any luck?" Ellie sat down beside Janet again. "Oh. That's not historical research."

"It's not," Janet agreed. "It's maybe related though."

"Why are you looking up Curtis?" Ellie asked. She narrowed her eyes and squinted at the screen. "I've never seen him with a beard before."

"You know him?"

"Sure. He's Tim Weber's brother. Well, half brother. Different dads, I guess. He was a lot younger, so we didn't cross paths at school, but I used to see him when I would hang out at Tim's house sometimes."

Janet nodded. She'd forgotten Ellie had dated Tim Weber for a while in high school. He was in Janet's class and played trumpet in the marching band, and half the flute section had a crush on him. Okay, if she was honest, Janet also had a small crush on him for a while, but obviously it hadn't gone anywhere.

"Do you know much about Curtis these days?"

"I ran into him at the gas station—the one by the medical center—a few weeks ago. He works there now." Ellie shrugged. "I think he got into some trouble a while back, but he seemed to be doing all right when I saw him."

"You mean when he broke into the auto parts store?"

Ellie nodded. "I read about it in the paper. It's really sad. Tim's mom worked so hard to keep those boys fed and out of trouble, but Curtis always found a way to test the limits, even as a kid. His dad wasn't much help, from what I understand, and Tim's dad was long gone, so I think she just did the best she could."

"Huh." Janet mulled this all over in her mind.

"Do you think Curtis could have been behind the break-in at your place?" Ellie asked.

"I don't know." Janet would never want to get his name mixed up in this if he wasn't responsible. But the police were the ones who had made the connection. "His name has come up."

"Well, I hope it isn't him, for his mom's sake. She was always kind to me."

Janet tried to recall Tim's mom's face and couldn't. "How is Tim these days?"

"Last I heard, he was living in Columbus and working at Ohio State. Married, a couple of kids. It seems like he managed to make a good life for himself."

"I'm glad to hear that," Janet said. "Maybe one of these days he'll make it back for a reunion."

"Maybe." Ellie shrugged. "Well, anyway, if you want to find Curtis, you could try at the gas station."

"Thanks. I just might," Janet said. She needed to get gas anyway.

"Let me know if you need anything else," Ellie said.

"I think I'm good." Janet logged out of the computer and pushed herself up. "Thanks for your help."

"Anytime."

Janet swung past the fiction section on her way to the front. She spotted a couple of mysteries that looked intriguing, so she took those to the circulation desk and checked them out, and then she headed back to her car. She planned to swing by the café to see how the painting was going, but before she did that, she would just pop in to the gas station and fill her tank and see if she could get a look at Curtis.

The gas station was on a corner lot, not far from the highway. Janet filled the tank, and then she made her way into the small convenience store attached to the garage. The aroma of hot dogs and motor oil and the sickly-sweet scent of the slushy machine greeted her as she stepped inside. The cracked linoleum floor was worn thin in places, the fluorescent overhead lights flickered dimly, and the shelves seemed to be stocked with mostly energy shots and beef jerky. Janet made her way to the front, where a big man in a hoodie was fooling with his phone behind the counter. Was it Curtis?

"Hi," Janet said.

"Yeah?" he drawled lazily. The man looked up slowly, and Janet felt a flash of recognition. This was the same face she'd seen on her screen, minus the beard.

Janet realized she hadn't figured out a cover story. She thought quickly. Behind the counter, there were shelves of cigarettes, cartons of chewing tobacco, and a display of lottery tickets. She didn't want any of those things. "I was looking for some...gum." Okay, that was a ridiculous thing to say. The gum was on her side of the counter, in plain sight.

"It's right there."

"Oh! Silly me." Janet pretended she hadn't seen it and grabbed a pack of mint gum. "Is this station open twenty-four hours?" It was another bad attempt at engaging, but at least it wasn't as bad as the first.

"Hours are on the door," he said, and looked back down at his phone.

She glanced over at the door. So they were.

"Oh, it closes at nine." She thought frantically through the next few seconds and finally blurted out, "So, do you like to go home right after work, or do you like to go somewhere and unwind?"

"Lady, did you need anything besides the gum?" Curtis repeated, frowning at her. He was not at all pleased with her questions.

"No, I think I'm gonna just skip it," she said. She put the gum down, and then she turned and walked out quickly. When she was outside, she ran to her car, threw it in gear, and drove away. She wasn't sure why she was in such a hurry. It wasn't as if he was following her. But it felt like he could, and if he did, it wouldn't go well.

Janet's heart rate didn't slow until she was at the café. She found Debbie working on the computer in the back and Jaxon rolling yellow paint over the graffiti.

"Oh, hi." Debbie glanced up as she walked in. "I told Jaxon to just cover the graffiti, not do a whole paint job. I hope that's okay."

"That's fine," Janet said. "It looks like he's making good progress."

"He says he'll finish up today."

"That's great. So we can open up tomorrow as usual?"

"I think so. Greg said it'll be a few days before the door gets fixed, but I think we can be back in business without that."

"I think so too." Well, that was a relief.

"What did you find?"

Janet filled Debbie in on what she'd learned about the briefcase theft as well as what she'd discovered about Curtis. "He was a little scary," she said. "But I have no clue whether he was behind it or not."

"Maybe you can find out from Ian tonight," Debbie said.

Janet wasn't so sure. "Ian doesn't usually talk about his work at home."

"Maybe he'll make an exception in this case, since it's the café."

"I'll see what I can find out."

After she filled Debbie in on the rest of the details, Janet asked if she wanted her to stick around.

"No, why don't you go on home," Debbie said. "Greg will be back to pick Jaxon up when he's done. I'll stay and lock up once they're gone."

"Are you sure?" Janet asked the question, but she smiled to herself, knowing Debbie would be more than happy to see Greg again.

"Really, I'll be fine," Debbie assured her. "It'll give me time to get all the paperwork filed with the insurance company. The sooner we get that done, the sooner we get reimbursed."

"All right." Janet wasn't going to argue with her about it. "I'll see you in the morning."

"Bright and early."

CHAPTER SIX

anet made a hearty beef and vegetable stew for dinner that night along with crusty rolls and a green salad, and as she and Ian ate, she asked him what he'd learned about the break-in so far.

"Janet, you know I can't talk to you about an open police investigation," he said.

It was the answer she'd expected. The answer he'd given every time she'd asked him about a case over the years they'd been married. But still. Surely, he could see that this case was different.

"I'm not asking you to tell me anything you shouldn't," she said. "Just, you know, whether you're close to figuring out who it was."

"No comment," Ian said. "How did it go cleaning up the café today?" He took a bite of stew.

"It was fine." She broke open one of the rolls and let the steam waft out. "It looks like we'll be able to reopen tomorrow."

"That's great news."

"Yes, it is." She slathered on butter and then tried again. "Did the security footage from the museum show anything useful?"

"I'm not going to talk to you about what was on the tape."

"Were you able to talk to Alyssa Brown?"

"I did speak with her," Ian said. "Can you pass the butter?"

Janet passed the butter. "And? Do you think she did it?"

"This sure is good stew. Is it a new recipe?"

"Debbie and I actually went by Glazed today," Janet said.

"You did?" That got his attention. "Why?"

"We wanted to see what she had to say."

"What she had to say?" Ian cocked his head. "Did you think she might suddenly confess to you?"

"No." Though it would have been nice if she had. "Like I said, we just wanted to see what she would say."

"Janet, I know this one is personal for you. Believe me when I say I get that," he said. "But this is an active police investigation. I can't have civilians inserting themselves into the middle of this case. Even if that civilian does happen to be my beautiful and charming wife, who makes the best beef stew in town."

"We didn't get into the middle of it. We just visited a neighboring bakery."

"Janet. This is serious. I mean it. The doughnut shop owner is the least of my worries. We don't know what happened in the café last night, and some of the possibilities we're investigating involve some dangerous characters."

"You mean Curtis Smollen?"

"How do you know about Curtis?"

"You mentioned him to Deputy Vaughn this morning." She saw Ian let out a slow breath. "I couldn't help overhearing." Well, she couldn't help it after she'd moved closer to him, anyway. "And what happened at the café is just like what happened at the auto parts store he robbed, isn't it?"

Ian sighed. "Curtis Smollen is one possibility. There are others. And trust me, you don't want to get mixed up with any of them. Please, Janet, leave this alone."

So he had another suspect in mind besides Curtis and Alyssa. She wanted to ask more about that, about who it was and why he thought they might be involved, but she knew better than to ask him right now. She could see he wasn't messing around. Good thing she hadn't mentioned her trip to the gas station to him yet. She'd have to tell him, but she would wait for a more opportune time.

"I'm asking you to stay out of this for your own safety," Ian said. "Understood?"

"Fine. Yes." She understood, even if she didn't like it.

"We will figure out who did this, and we'll make sure they are held accountable," Ian said. "I can promise you that. I just need you to leave this to us in the meantime."

"All right," she said. She took a bite of her roll and thought through everything she'd learned since the break-in.

"Just one more question," she said. "And then I'll drop it."

"What is it?" Ian sounded weary.

"What do you think about the idea that whoever broke in wasn't really after the money in the register?" She set the roll on her plate. "What if the picture that was taken was what they were after all along?"

"I think that seems extremely unlikely, given the leads we have."

"Why?"

"No comment."

"We found out today that the picture that was stolen might actually be really important," Janet continued. "It contains a clue to an old unsolved mystery."

"Oh yeah?" He didn't buy it, but he was listening.

Janet told him what she knew about the old briefcase theft, and Ian nodded.

"So Debbie and I were wondering if maybe the picture was the point after all," Janet said. "And the rest was just misdirection."

"It's an interesting idea," Ian said. "But again, given what we suspect, and the people who we think might be involved, I'd say the chances are slim to none that the intended point of the theft was an old picture."

"And what is it you suspect?"

"Nice try." Ian shoveled more stew into his mouth.

Janet saw that she wasn't going to get anything more out of Ian right now. Why was he so convinced it wasn't about the picture? What did he know he wasn't telling her?

He'd asked her not to get mixed up in it, but she couldn't help but want to find out.

CHAPTER SEVEN

*J*anet went into the café the next morning at the regular time. The top panel of the door was still covered with plywood, but the walls were once again a smooth, uniform lemony yellow. This afternoon they could rehang the pictures, and the space would be nearly as good as new. The place still smelled like paint fumes, but once she got the muffins baking and the coffee brewing, hopefully no one would notice that.

Janet pulled the CLOSED FOR REPAIRS sign off the door, started a fresh pot of coffee, and then got working on the morning's baking.

Debbie was a little late coming in and had to rush to get the front of the café ready for customers. Janet had just left the kitchen to get another cup of coffee when Patricia Franklin walked in.

"Hello," she said. "I'm glad to see you all are back at it."

Janet smiled. "Hi, Patricia. We were grateful that the damage wasn't very extensive." Debbie moved over to the espresso machine and started steaming the milk for Patricia's regular order, a peppermint mocha.

"Did they catch whoever who did this?" Patricia asked.

"Not yet. But they're working on it," Janet said.

"Well, let's hope they catch him soon," Patricia said. They chatted about the work of rehanging the pictures while Debbie brewed the espresso and added peppermint syrup, chocolate, and whipped cream to the drink.

"Thank you," Patricia said when Debbie handed her the cup. "I can't stay—I have a deadline this morning on a case I'm working on, but tell my grandfather I said hello and rub Crosby's ears for me."

Janet waved her off and got her own cup of coffee.

Everyone who came into the café seemed really excited that they'd opened again so quickly. Janet was glad to see that their regular customers had come back. They'd lost a day of sales, but hopefully they'd make up for it today.

Once the rush died down, Janet peered out the window and saw exactly what she'd been hoping for. Harry sitting on his bench on the train platform, Crosby at his feet. Other than the special event trains sponsored by the depot museum, no trains stopped in Dennison these days, although freight trains used these rails and went past several times a day. Harry and Crosby liked to sit and watch them go by.

Janet made some scrambled eggs, spooned them onto a paper plate, and poured plain black coffee into a to-go cup. She called to Debbie, "Do you mind if I go talk to Harry for a minute?"

Debbie looked up from the table she was busing. "Not as long as you tell me whatever he says."

"I will," Janet promised. She walked outside to the bench where Harry sat. He wore a thick wool coat, with the collar turned up against the stiff wind, and a red knit hat.

"Hi, Harry. I brought you some coffee. And, of course, some eggs for Crosby." She set the plate on the platform, and Crosby leaned forward and started to eat.

"Hi, Janet." He ducked his head. "You didn't have to do that."

"By the way, Patricia says hi. How are you?" Janet sat on the bench next to him. She handed him the coffee, and he took it gratefully.

"Oh, I'm doing fine, all things considered," he said. "I figure when you get to be my age, any day you're still walking around is a good day."

Harry was ninety-five years young. He'd started working at the train station as a porter when he was just fifteen, in the midst of the war. He'd gone on to be a conductor, riding the rails up and down the Pittsburgh, Cincinnati, Chicago & St. Louis Railway lines.

"And how are you, Crosby?" Janet rubbed the dog's ears.

"Spoiled," Harry said with a laugh. "But that's the best way for a dog to be, isn't it?"

"It is." Janet agreed. "Harry, I have a question about something that happened here at the station during the war."

"Well, I don't know if I'll remember it, but if I do, I'll help you out."

"Do you remember when a briefcase full of money went missing?" Janet asked.

"Oh yes." Harry nodded and took a sip of his coffee. "I do remember that day."

"What happened?"

"Well, it was, what, maybe 1945 or so?"

"1944," Janet said. "November."

"That sounds right. Well, everyone talked about this big ceremony for weeks. Wilbur Finnegan was going to donate ten thousand dollars to the hospital. Which always struck me as kind of odd, if you want to know the truth."

"Why?"

"Wilbur was kind of a big man in town, I guess you would say."

"Why was that?"

"He built that big yellow Victorian over on Fourth Street. The one with all the gables?"

Janet knew the one he was talking about. It was one of the most beautiful and ornate houses in town. "He must have been doing quite well for himself."

"Wilbur owned the bank. Finnegan Bank and Trust. It was bought out by one of those chains decades ago, but back then, if you wanted to borrow money to buy a house or anything like that, you had to talk to Wilbur."

Something in the way he said it made Janet understand that Harry had not been Wilbur's biggest fan. "You didn't like him?"

Harry shrugged. "I didn't know him. I was just a kid."

"But?"

"But he had a way of finding reasons not to lend to certain people, I guess you might say," Harry said. "And considering how wealthy he was, he sure didn't do much for the war effort."

"But he gave ten thousand dollars for the hospital."

"Sure, but we'd been in the war for almost three years by the time he did it. It seemed he put it off for as long as he could get away with. Meanwhile, everyone else in town rationed sugar and butter, sending sons and brothers off to the front lines, and there was Wilbur, going on as usual, driving his big old Packard, his grown sons right there beside him."

"I heard they had medical exemptions."

Harry smiled grimly. "He had two strong sons, but miraculously, they were both granted medical exemptions. Something about their hearts. That didn't stop them from working for their dad though." He took another sip. "While everyone else scrimped and saved and gave up everything extra for the war effort, making do with coats that were too small and shoes that had holes, Wilbur would come back from shopping trips to Chicago loaded down with boxes of new clothes."

"Wow. How do you know all this?"

"I unloaded his trunks and bags and cases from the first-class carriage," Harry said.

That made sense. As a porter, Harry probably saw all kinds of things people didn't realize he saw. Janet had rarely heard Harry talk like this about anyone. Wilbur must have been a real unsavory character if the always affable Harry disliked him.

"How do you know he didn't help the war effort quietly?" Janet asked. "Maybe he did, but no one knew about it. Maybe it was a right hand doesn't know what the left hand is doing kind of thing."

Harry laughed. "It's entirely possible. I guess only the Lord knows, and that's as it should be. But Wilbur wasn't one to do things quietly. If he was going to do something good, he made sure people knew about it. Which is why when Mayor Humphreys finally wore him down and convinced him to make a donation, he didn't just hand over the money, like most people would. He had to have a ceremony to highlight his generosity."

"Were you there when the money actually went missing?" Janet asked.

"I was at the station, sure. I wasn't anywhere near the photo shoot they'd set up though. I was over at that end of the station." He gestured to the museum. "There was a little room where the porters would wait between trains. The ceremony was set up over there." He gestured toward the grassy area in front of the café. "I saw them setting things up, positioning the briefcase to get just the right shot of it. Wouldn't want to give away money without it making the front page of the paper, now would you?"

Again, she marveled at how much it would take to provoke someone like Harry to speak like this even all these years later.

"When did you realize something had gone wrong?"

"Well, the cannon caught my attention first. Then people started yelling, saying someone stole the money."

"Do you know who noticed it missing first?" Janet asked.

"No, like I said, I wasn't anywhere near where the excitement was happening. But that doesn't mean I wasn't questioned."

"The police questioned you? Why, if you weren't anywhere near the cash?"

Harry gave her a wry smile. "All the porters were questioned. Probably everyone else was too."

"I read that the only people near the money at the time the briefcase was stolen were the three women posing for the photos and Wilbur himself."

"That sounds like what I heard as well," Harry said. "But who can say, really? Like I said, I wasn't there."

Janet nodded and thought about what he'd said. She thought about how to phrase what she really wanted to ask. "Do you think one of the women posing with the money might have taken it?"

"I don't see how. Not with all those eyes on them and that briefcase."

"But someone did manage to take it," Janet said. "*Someone* was able to get it away, even with all those eyes on them."

"Someone did," Harry confirmed. "And I don't think it was one of those girls."

Janet wondered if she was understanding what he wasn't saying. "Do you think there's a chance Wilbur took the briefcase himself?"

Harry shrugged. "I'd be lying if I said it never crossed my mind."

"You mean, you think he might have made a big show of donating the money and then taken it back and acted like it was stolen?" It was a devious idea. One that, if true, spoke very poorly of Wilbur. Actually, the fact that Harry even thought it was a possibility spoke poorly of Wilbur.

"How would that have worked?" she asked.

"Can't say for sure." He shrugged. "But if the only people near the briefcase when it went missing were the three girls and Wilbur, well, one of them must have done it. And would you be more likely to assume it was stolen by one of the girls who volunteered their time and energy to help feed hungry soldiers during the war, or the rich banker who had to be shamed into contributing to the war effort at all and made no secret of the fact that he wasn't at all happy about parting with his cash?"

"I see your point." It didn't mean Wilbur was behind it, necessarily, but if those were the four possibilities, it did seem that he should be considered.

"Was Wilbur ever questioned?"

"I don't know." He shrugged again. "They weren't exactly sharing information with me. I was just a porter. All I know is that if I had to pick a direction to look, that's where I would have started."

Janet nodded. It was a good suggestion. But how would one investigate something like that now?

"What happened to the Finnegans? When did they leave town?" Janet had never met anyone with that last name around Dennison.

"Wilbur moved to Chicago when he sold the bank. I think it was sometime in the sixties, maybe? I don't know for sure." Harry sipped his coffee and patted Crosby, who had settled at his feet. "But Wilbur's daughter still lives around here, I think. She's a bit younger than the sons."

"Norma. She lives in Columbus. I already reached out to her."

"It sounds like you're ahead of me." Harry took another sip. "It's good that you're interested in this. Wouldn't it be something if you could find out what happened after all this time?"

It would indeed, Janet thought. She just hoped she'd be able to do it.

CHAPTER EIGHT

*P*aulette Connor showed up just before the midday rush.

"It's just like new in here," she said, nodding at the freshly painted walls.

"Except for the plywood on the door," Janet said.

"Greg will get that fixed up before you know it." Paulette waved her concern away. Paulette was Greg's mother, and she waited tables at the café a few hours a day. "Jaxon did a great job, didn't he?" She slid an apron around her neck and tied the strings behind her back.

"He did," Debbie said.

"Are you going to have him help you rehang the photos?" Paulette asked. "He can handle that."

Janet looked at Debbie. "That's a good idea," she said.

Debbie nodded.

The first lunch customers showed up not long after that, and while Debbie and Janet made sandwiches and dished out potato salad and desserts, Paulette chatted with the customers.

"Janet?"

Janet glanced up and was surprised to see her dad standing in front of her. "Oh. Hi, Dad." She looked around. "Is Mom with you?" It was rare to see the two of them apart since his retirement.

"I told her I had to run out and buy food for the fish." He held up a paper bag stamped with the logo from the local pet store. "She hates the way that place smells, so I knew she wouldn't want to come."

"Don't you have, like, two full containers of fish food?" Janet had seen them on the shelf below the tank that burbled in their living room.

"Your mother never feeds the fish. She won't know that."

"Okay. Are you here for lunch?"

"No, I wanted to talk to you about the party. I asked your mom what kind of food she likes at parties, and she said just normal, everyday food. Nothing fancy."

"You asked Mom about party food?" Janet cocked her head. "Isn't this party a surprise?"

"I didn't tell her it was for an actual party," Dad said. "Just hypothetically."

"Oh. Okay." Janet stifled a smile. She couldn't imagine that her mom hadn't seen right through that, but what did she know? "So you're saying you don't want anything fancy."

"That's right. Maybe fried chicken, mac and cheese, some of those little crab balls she liked so much at Maryann's wedding."

Janet could call her cousin Kelly. Maybe she would remember where the recipe for the crab balls had come from.

"How about I put together a potential menu and run it past you?" she suggested.

"That sounds great. Thanks, honey."

"No problem, Dad. You'd better get home before Mom starts to get suspicious."

Dad nodded, held up his bag of fish food, and turned and walked out of the café. Janet thought about the party for a few moments and realized she should think about a gift for her parents. What did you give someone to celebrate fifty years together? What could possibly be meaningful to them? Especially since her mom hated clutter and was always trying to give away the things she had. Maybe an experience of some kind. A gift certificate for a dinner out? They did like that Italian place. She thought about photos. A scrapbook of some kind? Maybe showcasing their fifty years together? But Mom already had their photos organized in albums. What about a slideshow? What if she digitized photos from their many years together and put together a slideshow, set to music? They would like that. She would need to get the photo albums from Dad, but he wouldn't know why she wanted them.

Her mind made up, Janet went back to serving customers. By one o'clock, the crowd had thinned out, and she and Debbie sent Paulette home while they finished cleaning up for the day.

"Oh, what a shame, we have a leftover chocolate chip scone," Debbie said, helping herself to the last one in the display case.

"Might as well eat it before it gets stale," Janet said as Debbie took a big bite. "Hey, are you headed straight home?"

"I don't have to be," Debbie said as soon as she'd swallowed the bite. "Do you have shenanigans in mind?"

"I don't know about shenanigans," Janet said. "But I was thinking I might stop by Good Shepherd again this afternoon."

"Definitely not shenanigans then," Debbie said. "But I don't have anything else pressing. Are you hoping to talk to Ray?"

"I am," Janet said, nodding. "I need him to tell me how to get in contact with Gayle."

"Let's go see him." Debbie grabbed the last of the day's muffins and tucked them into a bag before they locked up the café.

"My car is still making that weird noise, so can we take yours again?" Janet asked.

"I thought you said Ian was going to look at it?"

"He was. He is. He's just been busy."

"Well, I don't mind driving," Debbie said. "Let's go."

They headed to Good Shepherd and parked in the same spot, chatted with Mary again, and then found Ray in the large dayroom in the middle of a game of chess. Ray's opponent was a bald man with thick eyebrows and big round glasses.

"We're sorry to interrupt," Janet said.

"All you're interrupting is me getting clobbered," Ray said. Janet studied the board and saw he was right—there were only a few white pawns, a knight, and the white king left on the board, while Ray's opponent still had most of his pieces. "Dean won't mind if I surrender. Will you, Dean?"

Dean looked dubious until Debbie held up the bag. "We can offer consolation muffins."

"Well, in that case, I guess you can take him," Dean said. Debbie handed him a pumpkin spice muffin and a napkin, and Dean seemed satisfied. Ray maneuvered his wheelchair to a corner of the room where groupings of couches and chairs were set around low tables.

"It will be quiet over here, and no one will bother us." Once Debbie and Janet were seated, he said, "Do you have any more of those muffins?"

Janet laughed as Debbie handed him the bag. Ray selected a blueberry crumble muffin and took a bite.

"So what brings you all here today?" Ray asked. "Another mystery?"

"Actually, yes," Janet said. She took out her phone and pulled up the photo of the stolen picture. "We're trying to find information about this day."

She handed the phone to Ray, and he looked down at it.

"That's Gayle," he said.

"That's what we were told," Debbie said.

"That's my kid sister all right." He swiped at the screen. "How do I make it bigger?"

Janet reached over and used two fingers to enlarge the photo for him. He gazed at it, a bemused smile on his face.

"We were hoping to talk to her about something that happened on the day the picture was taken. Would you be able to put us in contact with her?"

"I sure can." He looked at the photo again. "I'm sure she'd be glad to talk to you. When was this picture taken? Can I help you with anything?"

"It was taken on November 11, 1944," Debbie said. "You weren't in Dennison then, were you?"

"No, I wasn't," Ray said. "I was still fighting in Europe." He turned to Janet. "Do you have a way to write down her phone number?"

"Sure." Janet opened a memo on her phone and waited. Ray also seemed to be waiting. "I'll make a note on my phone," she clarified quickly.

"Ah." Ray nodded. "I see. Okay." He rattled off a phone number from memory, and Janet typed it into her app.

"Wow. Not many people know phone numbers from memory these days," Debbie said.

"She's had the same number since the seventies," Ray said. "Back when you had to actually dial it."

"Thank you for your help," Janet said. "We'll give her a call."

CHAPTER NINE

*A*fter they'd said goodbye to Ray and popped in to give their regards to Eileen, Debbie drove back to the café, where Janet had left her car. But as they pulled into the small lot, she saw—

"Is that Alyssa?" Debbie leaned forward. Whoever it was had her nose pressed against the glass of one of the café's windows, her hands cupped around her eyes, peering inside. She wore jeans and a sweatshirt, and curly hair the same shade of fiery red as Alyssa's spilled out from under the hood.

"It does look like her," Janet agreed. She parked the car, and they both jumped out and hurried toward the figure.

"Hello?" Debbie called.

The person whipped around. Alyssa. She hadn't expected to see them, that was clear from her face.

"What brings you here?" Janet tried to keep her voice natural, but inside, she was shaking.

"Oh. Hello," Alyssa said. "How are you guys?"

"We're fine," Debbie said.

"I was just wondering how you two were doing, with the café closed," Alyssa said. She adjusted the strap on her tote bag, and Janet saw the bandage on her wrist that Debbie had pointed out.

"We were actually able to open up again this morning," Janet said. "Aside from the door, we're good as new."

Alyssa waited a beat too long before she said, "I'm so glad to hear it."

"We're very grateful," Debbie said. And then, when Alyssa didn't answer, she said, "Did you need something?"

"No, I really just came by to see how you were doing."

"Oh. Well, we're doing fine. Thank you so much for stopping by."

"Sure thing." Alyssa stood there awkwardly for a moment longer, and then she waved and moved off toward the parking lot. They watched as she climbed into a beat-up Prius that was plastered with bumper stickers.

After she drove off, Janet said, "That was weird, right?"

"Definitely," Debbie said.

"Why was she here?"

"And why did she say she came to see us when the café is closed? She's been here enough to know our hours."

Janet nodded. "Guess who just moved right back up to the top of the suspect list?"

Janet made a white bean and kale soup with sausage for dinner. On a cold night like tonight, it filled the kitchen with warmth and delicious scents. She popped some frozen rolls into the oven again and tried not to be sad that there were only two on the baking sheet. Tiffany was having a good time at college, she knew that. But, since she had a few minutes before Ian would get home, maybe she'd give Tiffany a call to see how she was doing. She took out her phone.

"Hey, Mom," Tiffany answered. Janet could hear lots of voices on the other end of the line. "I'm just heading into the dining hall."

"Oh good. What's the special tonight?" When Janet and Ian were there for parents' weekend, they had been served a delicious roast beef.

"I don't know yet. Hang on." She said something Janet couldn't understand to someone, and then she came back. "Can I call you later, Mom? I'm meeting my roommate, and I'm trying to grab us a table."

"Okay. Have fun. I miss you."

"Bye."

Janet was glad Tiffany was doing well and settling in at school. *That's the best possible scenario*, she reminded herself. She was learning to navigate life without her parents, and that was a good thing.

But that didn't mean Janet didn't miss her every single day.

She decided this would be a good time to give Gayle a call. She looked up the number she'd entered for Gayle and dialed.

"Hello?" Gayle sounded wary. Janet was impressed that she'd even picked up. Most people these days didn't answer calls from numbers they didn't recognize.

"Hi, Gayle. This is Janet Shaw," Janet said. "From Dennison?"

"Hello!" Gayle's voice softened. "How are you, Janet?"

"I'm doing just fine. How are you?"

"Not too shabby." At ninety-one, Gayle still had more energy than Janet did most days.

"I hope you don't mind me calling. Ray gave me your number."

"I don't mind at all. I'm delighted to hear from you."

"Oh good. I'm actually calling because of... Well, it's sort of strange. I have some questions about a photograph that was taken at the depot back in 1944. You're in the photograph, along with two other women."

"Is that right?"

"The thing is, it was taken, from what I understand, just before a large amount of money was stolen in a briefcase."

"Oh, you mean the day the cannon went off and someone escaped with Wilbur Finnegan's donation money?"

"That's right."

"My goodness. I haven't thought of that day in years."

"Would you be able to tell me about it?"

"Oh, sure. But it's a long story, and I don't have much time right now. I'm about to head out to my aqua aerobics class. Why don't you stop by sometime, and I can tell you about it?"

"I..." Janet wasn't sure what to say. Gayle lived in Columbus. She could hardly just stop by. But she did want to hear this story. "Sure. When is good for you?"

"How about tomorrow?"

"Would the afternoon work?" Janet asked. If she and Debbie went after they closed up shop, they could make it there and back before it got too late.

"Sure. I'm free all day." Gayle gave Janet her address. After she hung up, Janet called Debbie and told her they were taking a quick trip to Columbus, and Debbie was game when she understood why.

Ian came home just as Janet took the rolls out of the oven.

"It smells good in here." A blast of cold air followed Ian into the house, but he closed the door quickly.

"It's almost ready."

While Ian washed up and Janet ladled the soup into bowls and set out the rolls and salad, she told him about her visit to Good Shepherd. After they said grace, she asked, "So, any news?"

"We're working on some leads," Ian said. "I promise we're trying our best to find the person who did this, Janet."

She believed him. But that didn't mean she wasn't anxious to hear what was happening.

"Do you have any new leads?" she asked.

"We're looking into a few possibilities."

"Like what?"

"Janet, I'm not going to talk to you about this." Ian's words were kind but firm. "This is an open investigation."

He wasn't going to give anything away. Janet knew she should just drop it. But she had to try one more time.

"Debbie and I found Alyssa Brown looking into the windows of the café this afternoon, well after the café closed."

"What?" Ian set his spoon down.

"It was really weird. Debbie and I went to talk to Ray Zink after we locked everything up, and when we came back to the café so I could pick up the car, Alyssa was there, looking into the front window."

"Did she say why she was there?" Ian asked.

"She made up a quick excuse about wanting to see how we were doing," Janet said. "But it was clear she was surprised to see us."

"And then what happened?"

"She left. And Debbie and I agreed the whole thing was very strange."

Ian nodded. "Thank you for letting me know."

That was it? He wasn't going to drop everything and call Alyssa and demand she come into the station?

"She has a cut on her wrist," Janet added. "Like she got cut on something sharp. We think it could be her blood on the piece of glass in the door."

"I'll look into it," Ian said, and took a bite. Watching him, Janet felt herself get more and more upset. How could he just sit there calmly eating soup when it was obvious that he should be contacting Alyssa?

"I think she's the one who broke into the café," Janet said.

"She's not the one who broke into the café." Ian tore his roll apart. A delicious scent wafted up.

"How do you know it wasn't her?" How could he be so sure?

Ian thought for a moment, and then he let out a breath. "The museum's security camera footage shows a man breaking into the café."

"Wait. What?" He'd seen something on the security camera footage and he hadn't told her? "When did you discover that?"

"We reviewed the footage yesterday," Ian said. "You can't see much. It's really blurry and dark. It's taken at night, from far away. We can't tell who the guy is. But it's clearly a man."

Janet let that sink in. "So it's not Alyssa?"

"It's not Alyssa, unless she happens to be over six feet, spends a lot of time lifting weights, and wears work boots."

"That doesn't sound like her," Janet said. She felt deflated. "But that doesn't mean she wasn't behind it. She could have had someone else do her dirty work, couldn't she?"

"She could have," Ian said. "That's why I was interested to hear about your interaction today. We'll investigate to see if that's a possibility. But as I told you yesterday, we're also looking into some other possibilities."

"Like what?" *Like Curtis Smollen*, she thought.

"I'm not going to tell you that," Ian said. He took a bite of his roll. "So, how's Ray doing?"

The conversation was over for now, he was saying. But that didn't mean it was done.

Janet was climbing into bed when she heard Ian's phone vibrate on his bedside table. He was in the bathroom, brushing his teeth. Janet glanced over, just to make sure the message wasn't anything urgent. It was from Deputy Vaughn. Work, then. Janet was about to lean back on her side of the bed, but she couldn't help reading the message that flashed onto the screen. HEARD FROM CPD. THERE'S A MEMBER OF THE KINGS IN DENNISON. BERNARD SAMPSON. WE CAN CONTACT HIM TOMORROW RE: CAFÉ.

This was about the break-in at the café. What was CPD? What was "the Kings"? Janet tried to make sense of the message, but it vanished as the screen went dark. She contemplated touching the screen to make it come back, but she didn't. This wasn't her business. She certainly wasn't going to violate Ian's privacy and his trust by going into his phone to read his text messages.

However, she knew that the message would reappear a minute or two after it first came in. If Ian stayed in the bathroom long enough, and if she leaned over so she could see it when it did…

The water turned off in the bathroom. She waited, poised to push herself back if Ian came out. Surely the message would pop up in another few seconds…

Aha. There it was. HEARD FROM CPD. THERE'S A MEMBER OF THE KINGS IN DENNISON. BERNARD SAMPSON. WE CAN CONTACT HIM TOMORROW RE: CAFÉ.

CPD. The Kings. Bernard Sampson. Janet made a mental note of these things and rolled over to her side of the bed just before Ian opened the bathroom door and came back into the bedroom.

"Good night," he said, climbing into bed.

"Good night." She leaned over and gave him a kiss. "Your phone vibrated while you were in there."

She did her best to act nonchalant, trying to pretend there was nothing out of the ordinary going on.

"Thanks." Ian picked up his phone and read the message, and then he put it back on his nightstand.

"I love you," he said. He turned off the light and rolled over.

Janet tried to drift off to sleep, but she kept thinking about the text message. What was CPD? What, or who, were the Kings? And who was Bernard Sampson? She had told Ian she would stay out of it and let him do his job. But she couldn't stop wondering, no matter how hard she tried.

Finally, she decided that she would have to do a tiny bit of research in the morning. She wouldn't get involved in the investigation. She would just see what she could find out, to see if it was important. With that decision made, she was finally able to drift off to sleep.

CHAPTER TEN

Thursday morning dawned cold, and a scrim of hazy clouds stifled the waning moonlight as Janet drove to the café. She had thought the seat and steering wheel warmers in her car were an extravagance she didn't need when they'd bought it, but now she was glad Ian had insisted.

As she brewed the coffee and mixed the ingredients for the day's baking—scones, croissants, a few dozen doughnuts—she thought through the message she'd seen on Ian's phone last night. She didn't know what the Kings were. Or who Bernard Sampson was. But she had a pretty good idea of what CPD was. *PD* stood for police department. She hadn't been married to a cop all these years to not recognize those letters. But which police department? Columbus? Chicago? Cincinnati? Cleveland? Canton? It could be any of them. She'd need to learn more.

When Debbie came in, Janet poured them each a big mug of coffee and updated her on what she'd learned last night.

"Kings?" Debbie's nose wrinkled.

"Does that mean something to you?" Janet asked.

"No. I just remembered there was a crown painted on the wall."

Janet pulled up the photos she'd taken of the scene on her phone and found the one that showed the crown. "Do you think the crown has something to do with the Kings?"

"I think it would make sense," Debbie said. "Though what it means, I don't know. Do you think Alyssa has some connection to crowns, or kings?"

"You mean, is she secretly royalty?" Janet smiled.

"More like, is there some hidden meaning that relates to her doughnuts? She's the queen of doughnuts, maybe?" Debbie shook her head. "Okay, even as I said that, I knew it sounded ridiculous."

"I've got news on the Alyssa front, actually," Janet said. She told Debbie about the figure in the footage being a man.

"So it wasn't Alyssa who broke in?" Debbie asked. She seemed as puzzled by the news as Janet had been.

"It was a man, apparently," Janet said.

"We need to get a copy of that security camera footage," Debbie said.

Janet hesitated.

"What?"

"I told Ian I would stay out of the investigation."

"You are staying out of it. You won't do anything about it. You just want to see it for yourself."

Janet understood Debbie's logic. But she still wasn't sure.

"How about I go ask Kim for a copy of the footage?" Debbie smiled. "That way, you can honestly say you had nothing to do with it."

Janet wasn't sure Ian would see it that way, but she had to admit she was very curious to see the footage for herself.

"If you happened to get a copy, I don't see how I could stop you from watching it around me," she finally said.

"I'll go over and visit Kim as soon as the museum opens," Debbie said.

Then Janet brought the conversation back to what she'd seen on Ian's phone.

"I'm pretty sure the message was about a police department, but I don't know about the other bits."

"Looks like we have some research to do," Debbie said.

They unlocked the doors, and soon the café hummed with activity. Things didn't slow down until midmorning, in the lull between the breakfast crew and the lunch crowd. When Janet got a few minutes, she opened her laptop and pulled up a search window.

She typed *membership Kings* into the search window, and—wow. Well, that search term was clearly too broad. She got the schedule for the Sacramento Kings basketball team, a college singing group, a bowling alley, a theater, even an ad for tickets to *The Lion King* on Broadway. This wasn't helpful, though she did like the idea of seeing a show on Broadway sometime. She added *CPD* to her search, and this yielded links to continuing Professional Development at King's College, London. She sorted through the links, and none of them had anything to do with the break-in.

Well, she would keep thinking on that one. She moved to her next search term and typed in *Bernard Sampson*. She hit enter.

She clicked on the first link that popped up and saw it was a social media profile, but the account was locked. That was no good.

There were a few links that referenced Bernards but none of them seemed to be the one she was looking for. And there was a link to—

Oh. There was a link to a site called Mugshots. Was this a real site? She read the notice at the top of the page. Apparently, this was a website dedicated to posting open records of arrests in order to inform the public.

She clicked on the link and then entered *Bernard Sampson* in the search box. She scrolled through the results, looking for one who had been arrested in an Ohio city that started with *C*. On the fourth page she finally found one. This Bernard Sampson had been arrested for possession with intent to distribute and a weapons charge. The mug shot had been taken five years ago and showed a man with ghostly pale skin that set off the dark circles under his eyes. His nose was crooked, his wide forehead scratched. The shoulder-length brown hair that framed his face was greasy, and he had a scraggly beard and unkempt mustache.

This was the guy Ian thought might have broken into the café? Janet got chills down her spine just thinking about it. She didn't know why Ian thought he might be connected. What would a criminal in Cleveland have to do with the tiny Whistle Stop Café in Dennison?

She clicked on other links, but none of them seemed to offer any new clues. She needed to get back to work. She'd heard Paulette arrive as well as several groups of customers. Debbie and Paulette would need her help. She would quickly check her email, just in case...

Aha. There was an email from Norma Starr. Wilbur's daughter. She clicked on it eagerly.

Hello,

Thank you for your email. I am always interested in talking about my father and his legacy. Your email didn't say that you are with the press. If you are, our standard press pack is attached, though I'm happy to give a quote for your article as well. Please note that if this is in regard to an application for a grant from the Finnegan Foundation, your application will be given a thorough review and all communication must take place through the channels laid out in your application materials. If you are still interested in speaking with me, please use the link below to schedule a time with our online scheduler.

Norma

Well, that wasn't exactly warm and fuzzy. It looked more like a standard generic response. Still, she did sound like she might be willing to talk. Janet clicked on the link at the bottom of the email and was taken to a page where she could select from an array of available times on Norma's calendar. She found an open slot for the next day at four thirty. Janet booked the meeting and soon after got a confirmation email with an address and instructions for how to get inside the security gate. Goodness. Security gate? What was this place? She saved the email and then closed the window and headed back out into the café to face the lunch rush. Maybe Norma would be able to tell her what had really happened to that money.

CHAPTER ELEVEN

*A*fter the café closed and they were done cleaning up, they still had a few minutes before they needed to leave for Columbus to meet with Gayle. Greg had come by to install the new glass that morning, so the door was as good as new, and Jaxon was scheduled to come by to rehang the photos. Paulette had agreed to stick around and wait for her grandson, so she drank a cup of coffee and had a cookie break while she caught up with her sister over the phone.

"How about we check out the security camera footage from the museum?" Debbie asked.

Janet really wanted to see what was on it for herself. And watching the footage wasn't getting involved any more than googling Bernard Sampson was. It wasn't like they, themselves, were going to go after whoever it was the camera showed.

They sat behind Debbie's laptop, and Debbie inserted the memory stick. A grainy black-and-white image popped up, and it took a moment for Janet to make sense of what she saw on the screen. There was mostly a lot of black, with some dots of white.

"This is the camera outside the museum," Debbie said. "Which means that the café is over here." She pointed to the left side of the screen.

WHISTLE STOP CAFÉ MYSTERIES

Janet vaguely saw what she was referring to, though she wasn't sure how they were supposed to see anything useful given the dark and grainy footage.

"Let's see what there is," Debbie said. She clicked on the little arrow at the bottom of the screen to start the footage. "Okay, it's a little clearer now that it's running."

It was a little clearer, but it was still really hard to make out much of anything. There was just the front of the museum, the tracks, and, at the far side of the screen, the outside of the café. A moth flew in front of the camera a few minutes in, so Janet knew the camera was running, but there was nothing else happening. Janet focused on the time stamp at the top of the screen.

"Do we know what time the break-in happened?" she asked.

"I don't," Debbie replied. The time stamp said 10:27.

"How about we watch it on quadruple speed? We'll slow it down if we notice anything."

Debbie agreed and sped up the video. After several minutes of nothing happening, she sped it up even faster.

"Wait, what's that?" Janet asked.

Debbie stopped the video. The time stamp said 1:23, and something had moved in the corner of the screen. It was a figure. He— and it sure seemed like it was definitely a he—walked in from the bottom of the screen, where the parking area was. He was a big man, wearing baggy pants, boots, and a hooded sweatshirt, and his face was turned away from the camera. The hood was pulled up, so they couldn't see what his hair was like.

It could be Curtis, Janet thought. The guy had the same build as Curtis, and he was wearing a hooded sweatshirt when she'd met him. Maybe it was him. But there was no way to know for certain.

"Is something written on the back of his hoodie?" Janet said, squinting.

"I think so." Debbie paused the footage, and they both looked at the screen. "Or else it's a design of some kind?"

"It's so hard to tell," Janet said. "I think something is definitely there though."

"Is it the Glazed logo?" Debbie squinted at the screen.

Janet wanted it to be. She wanted it to be that simple. But she honestly couldn't tell. "I don't know."

"Why don't we keep going and see if it gets any clearer." Debbie hit play again, and they watched as the figure sneaked toward the café and paused, sizing up the side and front of the building. Then he walked up to the front door, took an object out of his pocket, and used it to smash the camera.

"What was that?" Debbie asked.

"It looked like a wrench or something," Janet said. "But it's hard to say for sure."

In the footage, the man put his gloved hand on the door handle. Finding it locked, he leaned forward and peered through the window in the top part of the door. Then, without hesitation, he smashed the glass using the same object. There was no sound in the video, but Janet could hear the sound of glass shattering in her head as she watched the pieces fall to the ground. He reached inside to unlock the door but pulled his hand back sharply and held it with his other hand.

"That's when he cut himself," Janet said, and Debbie nodded. That explained the spot of blood on the glass shard that remained in the door. He nursed his wound for about fifteen seconds, and then he reached inside the door again, avoiding the shard this time, and unlocked the door. Then he pushed it open and stepped inside. The lights inside the café flickered on, but Janet couldn't see what was going on once he was through the door.

"This is when he was flipping over tables and trying to jimmy the cash register open," Debbie said.

"And stealing the photo and spray-painting all over the walls," Janet added.

"Let's see how long it actually takes him," Debbie said. He emerged from the café at 1:37, holding the framed picture under his arm.

"He should be facing toward the museum's camera anytime now," Debbie said, but for the brief second he actually did face the camera, he was looking down, and his hood and the darkness obscured any chance they had of making out details. It was only as he was about to walk out of the bottom of the screen that they got a glimpse of him in profile.

"Pause it," Janet said. She studied the shape of the face, but it was too dark to really make out anything at all.

"Well, there's our guy," she said.

"Too bad there's no way to tell much about him," Debbie said. "Let's go to the shot where you can see that there's a design on his sweatshirt." She backed the footage up, and they watched as he walked toward the café again.

"Something is definitely there," Janet said. "It's just that it's so grainy and dark you can't tell what it is."

"Do you know if the police are going to get the video enhanced so they can analyze it better?" Debbie asked.

"I don't know if they're doing that or not," Janet said. "Ian didn't say anything about it."

Debbie was quiet for a moment.

"What are you thinking?" Janet asked.

"I was thinking about my neighbor, Zack Abbot."

"Zack?"

"He's in high school. He's really into making videos. He has his own social media page where he assembles Legos."

"You're kidding," Janet said. "Do people watch videos about Legos?"

"There are a lot of them, apparently. People make a living off advertising and sponsorships while they assemble Legos."

"I will never understand the world."

"I don't get it either, but here's my point. He has a lot of high-tech video equipment. He once showed me what he does to clean up videos, and it's like magic."

"And you're wondering if he would be able to help us with our footage," Janet said.

"Precisely." Debbie nodded. "Would you be okay with me giving him the file and seeing what he can do with it?"

"Sure." It couldn't hurt to get a better look at the guy on the screen. Zack probably didn't have equipment that could rival what the police had access to, but it would be interesting to find out whether he could help them.

"Great. I'll give it to him tonight." Debbie pulled the memory stick out of the computer. "In the meantime, we should get going."

Janet glanced at the clock and saw that it was indeed time for them to start the drive to Columbus. They said goodbye to Paulette, who promised to lock up, and as they drove through the downtown area, Janet noticed that the town had already started to put up the Christmas decorations that would adorn the light posts and hang over the streets. Thanksgiving was still two weeks away, and as much as she loved Christmas, she wanted to enjoy the beauty of this season. Still, she supposed it took a while to hang all the decorations.

As they left town, they passed the garden center, the home improvement store, and the strip of car dealerships, their signs high in the air—Chevrolet, Ford, Toyota, Master, Volkswagen. Janet always wondered how the people in the twin cities of Dennison and Uhrichsville were buying enough cars to support all those dealerships.

Once they were out of town, the landscape turned to farmland. The acres and acres of wheat and corn and soybean plants that lined the highway had mostly already been harvested, and large round bales of wheat dotted some of the fields.

It wasn't long before they arrived on the outskirts of Columbus and found their way to the Old Towne East district of the city, with its beautiful brick buildings and historic homes, some as old as the 1830s, lining the streets. Gayle's house was a one-story Victorian-style home painted a cheery yellow with white gingerbread trim.

Janet parked in front of the house, and they walked up the porch steps and rang the bell. A few moments later, Gayle opened the door.

"You made it. It's so good to see you." Gayle smiled and ushered them inside the house, which had stained oak floors and high ceilings. The walls of the hallway were papered in a vibrant floral pattern and featured elaborately framed paintings of the countryside. Gayle had a cast on her wrist, which had been broken in a car accident while visiting her brother in Dennison last month. She ushered them into what must have once been the home's formal parlor, with pressed tin ceilings and crenellated molding. A large fireplace topped with a marble mantel stood against one wall, and a cheery fire burned in the hearth. Big front windows let in lots of light, even on this gray day.

Gayle took a seat in a chintz armchair by the fire and gestured for them to sit on the club chairs. A plate of cookies and a pitcher of lemonade sat on a coffee table in front of her.

"It's so good to see you again," Debbie said. "How is your recovery coming along?" She nodded to Gayle's wrist.

"I'll be good as new and throwing this thing away before you know it," Gayle replied, fingering the cast. "Thanks for asking. But enough about me. That's not what brought you all this way. And I'd love to see that photograph you mentioned." Gayle scooted to the edge of her chair as Janet pulled the picture up on her phone and handed it over.

"Oh my," she said. A look Janet couldn't read passed over her face—recognition? Sadness? "How could I forget that day?"

"You remember it?" Debbie asked.

"Of course," Gayle said. "That was the day the hospital money was stolen from right under our noses."

"We'd love to hear about it," Debbie said.

"Well, I volunteered at the depot as often as I could back in those days. Pretty much everyone did. Giving out food and kindness to the young men who stopped at the depot on their way off to war felt like the least we could do."

"Was it hard, seeing so many young men shipping out to an uncertain future?" Janet asked.

"Oh sure," Gayle said. "They were just boys, really, and they had to say goodbye to everything they knew. But they were brave, and they did it willingly. It was better when we got trainloads of men coming home. They were battered and broken in so many ways, but they were always in good spirits because they were on their way home. Those trains were rare, though, at least until the end of the war."

"It must have helped them immensely to experience such warmth and encouragement along the way," Janet said.

"I hope so." Gayle smiled. "Anyway, the day of the theft was strange from the beginning. Everyone was really excited about the donation, of course. Wilbur Finnegan was finally giving to the war effort, and in a big way, so they made a whole thing out of it."

"We've heard that Wilbur had a reputation for not being the most generous person around," Janet said.

Gayle laughed. "That's a nice way of saying he was cheap, and you're right. So many people asked him for donations over the years, and he would always refuse. It became almost a joke in town—the richest man around gave the least to help the war effort."

"But he did finally make a donation," Debbie said. "And a sizeable one at that. Do you know why he changed his mind?"

"I don't suppose anyone really knows for sure," Gayle said. "But there were rumors, weren't there?"

"What do you mean?" Debbie leaned in.

"Well, like I said, I don't know for sure, but there were whispers about a car accident."

"A car accident?" Janet didn't understand where this was going.

"One of Wilbur's sons—Jasper, I think—had a dark blue Cadillac that he drove all over town. One day, some people who lived out on 250 reported hearing a crash and seeing his Cadillac in a ditch alongside the road. Jonas Wilkerson—he lived right along there—said he heard the crash and went out to see if he could help, and to his dying day he swore that there was a young woman in the car with Jasper when he got there, and she was in a bad way. But Jasper denied all of it—the crash, the neighbor, the woman. He said it was all made up."

"You mean…" Janet couldn't bring herself to say the words that had formed in her mind.

"No one knows what happened to the young woman, if she really did exist," Gayle said. "And the car vanished after that. No one ever saw it around town again. If there was an accident, it was swept under the rug."

"So the rumor was that Wilbur donated the money to the hospital because of the woman?" Debbie was clearly also trying to make sense of this.

"The suspicion was that her family insisted on the donation or they would tell what happened," Gayle said.

"So it was hush money," Janet said.

Gayle shrugged. "It was just a rumor. Never verified, to my knowledge. But that was what people said at the time."

"Why wouldn't the young woman's family want the money paid to them though? Why insist he make a donation to the hospital?" Janet asked.

"Who's to say they didn't want it? We don't really know. All I know is that Wilbur would have done anything to keep his precious sons out of trouble. That's why they were in town instead of off fighting the war in the first place," Gayle said.

"We heard they had medical exemptions," Debbie said.

"Oh sure." Gayle nodded. "All it took was a large check to a doctor in Cincinnati, and suddenly those men had bad hearts. It was amazing, really, that no one noticed how bad off their hearts were, considering. They were very nearly at death's door, by the sound of it." Gayle shrugged. "Though, when I'm feeling slightly more charitable, I can sort of understand that one. By all accounts, Wilbur had a terrible time of it in the First World War. Saw his friends gunned down, nearly died himself. You can understand a father trying to spare his sons that."

Janet had to admit she could. She could understand a parent wanting to protect his child from something as horrendous as war.

"But he can't have been the only veteran who didn't want his sons to go to war," Debbie said. "And yet it sounds like he was the only one in Dennison who bought their way out of it."

"Maybe he was the only one with the means," Gayle said. "I don't know. All I know is that they were around and that shortly after the rumored crash, Wilbur was suddenly making a huge donation to the hospital."

"We've heard the idea that Wilbur was actually the one who took the money," Debbie said. "After all, he was one of only a handful of people around when the briefcase went missing."

"That was definitely a theory that was floating around at the time," Gayle agreed. "And it may be true, I don't know. But then other people said that Wilbur couldn't have taken it, because he was so scared by the noise of the cannon that he had a panic attack and there was no way he could have grabbed the briefcase in the midst of that."

"It sounds like you don't believe that though," Janet said.

"Truthfully? I don't know," Gayle said. "I wouldn't put it past him to find a way to steal his own money back, but I don't know how he could have. That panic attack was real, from what I saw. Still, I wasn't watching him or looking at the briefcase. Like everyone else, I was trying to figure out what the noise was and whether we were under attack. So when that cannon went off, there was a lot of chaos."

Janet could only imagine. A loud boom in a crowd. People must have been terrified, trying to figure out what had happened and whether they were in danger. In all the confusion, anyone could have grabbed the briefcase and escaped without anyone else noticing.

"What do you think happened?" Debbie asked.

"I don't know for sure," Gayle said. "But if you want to know the truth, I've always assumed it had to be Dorinda."

"Dorinda?"

"She's the one on the right in that photo." Gayle pointed at the image on the phone's screen.

"Weren't all three of you cleared?" Janet asked.

"We were all considered suspects," Gayle said. "I don't know if any of us were ever officially cleared."

"What makes you think it was Dorinda?" Debbie asked.

"Because she was dating Jamison Finnegan," Gayle said. "I know these days it's frowned upon to assume women always do things for love, but I think she did it for love."

"So…" Janet tried to wrap her head around this. Had Jamison and Dorinda worked together to get the briefcase? "You think they came up with a plan together? Dorinda was selected for the photo, and—"

"If by 'selected,' you mean Jamison made sure she was there, then sure," Gayle said. "That's why she got picked to be in the photo, of course. She hardly ever volunteered at the canteen. But Jamison Finnegan wanted her in the photo, so there she was. At the time, we all assumed she just wanted to be in the papers. She was always going on about wanting to be a star, how she was going to get into modeling, and all that. But afterward, we started wondering if there was more to it."

"You think she might have been placed there strategically," Janet said. "So she would be close enough to take the briefcase when the moment arose."

"Do you think they planned to have the cannon go off?" Debbie asked.

"No, I don't think anyone could have planned for that," Gayle said. "And given how it caused Wilbur to react, I don't think his son would have been behind that happening. But I do think they were hoping for a strategic moment and they took advantage of it when it came."

"And after she grabbed the briefcase in all the confusion after the cannon went off, what would she have done with it?" Janet asked.

"Handed it off to someone, I assume," Gayle said. "Maybe Jamison himself, or maybe Jasper? But no one could tie them to the theft."

"The police interviewed them, I'm guessing?" Debbie asked.

"Oh yes, I'm sure they did. I know they interrogated Dorinda thoroughly. They interrogated all of us, naturally. The four of us—Jean, Dorinda, Wilbur, and I—really were the only ones who were close enough to the briefcase to have taken it, you see, so they knew it had to be one of us. Dorinda was the only one who made sense."

Janet thought all this through. "Was it a serious relationship between Jamison and Dorinda?"

"Oh, I don't know. I suppose in those days everything felt serious. But they didn't end up together, if that's what you mean. He dumped her shortly after that, from what I recall. I read that he ended up marrying some English woman after the war and moving to London. I don't really know."

"So if she helped him steal the money back for love, it didn't help her," Debbie said.

"But what if she didn't do it for love?" Janet asked.

They both turned and stared at her.

"What if it wasn't love that made her do it?" Janet tried again. "What if it was greed?"

"You think the Finnegans gave her a cut of the money once they had it back?" Debbie asked.

"It's possible," Gayle said.

"Whatever happened to Dorinda?" Janet asked. If she'd suddenly bought a house or shown in some way that she'd come into money, that might be a sign they were on to something.

"I don't know," Gayle said. "She moved away before the war ended, I think. I don't know where she went. Like I said, she hardly ever volunteered at the canteen, so I never really kept up with her."

Janet glanced at Debbie. It seemed like they would need to see what they could find out about Dorinda Meyer.

"What about Jean?" Debbie asked. "She's the third one in that photo, right?"

"That's right." Gayle nodded. "But it couldn't have been Jean. She was way too honest. She would never have taken it."

"Are you sure? Ten thousand dollars is a lot of money," Janet said. "It would tempt a lot of honest people."

"Not Jean," Gayle said. "She played piano at church, taught Sunday school, and gave away most of what she had. She ended up working as a nurse, taking care of the sickest babies in the neonatal intensive care unit. If she'd had ten thousand dollars, she would have donated it right back to the hospital to help those babies. I don't think there's any chance it could have been Jean."

Janet mulled this over. It wasn't proof that Jean was in the clear, but Gayle seemed pretty sure. So for now they would focus on Dorinda.

She looked at the picture on her phone again, and something occurred to her.

"What about the photographer?"

"What about him?" Gayle cocked her head.

"He was obviously close to the briefcase. Could it have been him?"

"He was close to the briefcase for a while, but not when the cannon went off. At that point he was taking pictures of the mayor, I think. I'm not sure. All I know is, after he finished taking pictures of us posing with the briefcase, he moved on. He definitely wasn't near us when the chaos ensued."

Janet nodded. It had been worth a shot.

"Can I ask what made you interested in the theft of the money after all this time?" Gayle asked.

Janet looked at Debbie. "It's a bit odd, really, if we're honest. The café was broken into a few nights ago."

"Goodness."

"The strange thing is, the only item that was taken was the photo from that day that we had hanging on the wall."

"Huh."

"We're trying to figure out if it was just random, or if there was a reason that photo in particular was stolen."

"If it wasn't random," Gayle said slowly, "if someone did take the picture on purpose, do you think that would mean they know something about the theft of the briefcase?"

"That's the theory we're working with," Janet said.

"In that case, the photo itself must contain some kind of clue about it," Gayle said. "Or why bother stealing it?"

"Perhaps someone knows what that photo represents, even if there's no clue in the photo itself," Debbie suggested.

Gayle was quiet for a moment. "Did you know the story behind the photo before it was stolen?"

"No," Janet and Debbie said at the same time.

"So stealing it only brought attention to it," Gayle said. "Yes, I think there must be a clue in the photo itself somewhere."

But what? "I wish we knew what it was."

Gayle shrugged. "If you can figure out who took that money way back when, I think there's a very good chance you'll find your recent thief. Though why it matters to someone after all these years, I couldn't say."

CHAPTER TWELVE

anet was making dinner. Well, technically, she was taking a quick break from making dinner while the hamburger and onions browned in the pan, and she was using her laptop to research "Kings" again. She'd tried a quick internet search on the name *Dorinda Meyer*, and it had gotten her nowhere, so she would need to do more in-depth research on her at the library. In the meantime, she was stuck on the Kings. She was sure it had something to do with that crown that had been spray-painted on the wall of the café, but she couldn't find anything online that helped her make a connection.

She was about to push herself up and return to the stove when her phone rang. *Tiffany*. Janet reached for the phone.

"Hey, Tiffany!"

"Hi, Mom."

"How are you? How did your classes go today?"

"Classes were fine," Tiffany said. "But I got a weird call from Grandpa."

"Oh, was he calling about the surprise party he's throwing Grandma for their anniversary?"

"So it is a surprise?"

"It is." Wait. "Isn't it?"

"I wasn't sure, because at one point during the conversation, I heard Grandma in the background. I think she was watching *Wheel of Fortune,* because she kept solving the puzzle."

"She was in the room with him when he called to invite you to the party?" That didn't make any sense.

"Maybe she wasn't in the same room. He could have been in the kitchen, I don't know." Janet's parents' house had a large open space on the first floor, with the kitchen and dining area right near the living room, where the television sat. "But if it's a secret, I thought it was weird that she was close enough that I could hear her."

"That is strange." What was Dad thinking? "Well, maybe she had headphones on or something. Or maybe he knew she was wrapped up in the show. You know how she can get—she's totally focused on whatever is right in front of her. Do you think you'll be able to make it to the party?"

"I'm going to try," Tiffany said. "I'll have to drive back the next day because I have classes Monday and Tuesday, but I'm hoping to drive down Saturday morning."

"I'm glad," Janet said. "Your grandparents will be so pleased."

"So how are you? What are you up to?"

"Right now I'm mostly banging my head against a wall." While she talked, she walked over and turned off the heat under the skillet. The meat looked brown enough.

"Sounds like a blast. What's going on?"

"I'm trying to figure out what a drawing of a crown means. I think it has something to do with something called the Kings." She gave the meat in the pan another stir. "To me it looks like just a generic crown, but your dad and Deputy Vaughn sure paid special attention to it."

"This is about the break-in? Dad told me about it. He said the thief took a picture off the wall?"

"Yes. Whoever it was spray-painted all over the walls, and in the space where the photo was, they painted a picture of a crown. And your dad and Deputy Vaughn took a lot of pictures of it. I'm trying to figure out how it relates—if it does—to something called the Kings."

"Did you try an image search? Maybe see if you can find an image like it?"

"What?"

"An image search. On the internet?"

"How do I do that?"

"Oh boy. This is going to be better than the time I showed you how to use the locator app."

"That one has been super useful." Janet had seen the app on her phone but didn't know what it was until Tiffany explained to her that it could show Tiffany's and Ian's locations. Well, technically, it showed her their phones' locations, but since they always had their phones with them, it was the same thing.

"Do a search using keywords, 'image search.'"

"Okay." Janet sat back down in front of her computer and did what Tiffany instructed. "A white screen comes up. There's a search bar in the middle of it."

"Click on the camera icon in the search bar then click on 'upload a file' and choose a photo from your computer."

"Any photo?"

"Sure. Anything you have handy, just so you can see how it works."

She clicked on the camera and the words *upload a file* and then navigated to her remote desktop and found a photo of Ranger wearing a bejeweled tiara. The tiara, from one of Tiffany's dolls, sat crooked on his head, and Ranger glared at the camera. Tiffany had loved to dress Ranger up when she was younger, and Ranger had to be the most patient cat in the world to put up with it. "I have a picture of Ranger wearing a tiara from a few years back."

"Oh. Wow. Why do you have that picture handy?"

"Because he looks so angry. It always makes me laugh."

"Okay, next time we're going to talk about cleaning out your files. But for now, go ahead and click on the picture."

"Done."

"Now what pops up?"

"Oh wow. To the left, it's the picture of Ranger. And to the right, there's a bunch of pictures of cats wearing tiaras." Oh goodness. "They're so cute. This is hilarious. I've never seen a collection of more angry cats. How does it find all those photos?"

"They're all pictures that people have posted online."

"And the internet somehow knows that my picture was of a cat wearing a tiara and finds all the corresponding photos across the web?"

"Yep."

Janet scrolled through the pictures. "Will it work the same way with the picture of this crown?"

"I don't know. Try it and see."

"Okay. Hang on." Janet emailed the photo to herself and then she went through the process of uploading it into the search bar.

"Oh wow." Could that—

"Did it work?" Tiffany asked.

"Oh goodness." That couldn't be right.

"Mom?"

She wasn't seeing this right.

"What did it turn up, Mom?"

"You'll never believe it."

CHAPTER THIRTEEN

"T he Kings is a *gang*?" Debbie said on the other end of the phone line.

"A gang based in Cleveland," Janet whispered. Ian was playing chess against a friend online after dinner, and he shouldn't be able to hear her, but Janet didn't want to take any chances, especially not after hearing about how her dad had acted on the phone with Tiffany. "And Bernard Sampson, who used to be in the gang, now lives in Dennison."

"Wait, wait. How did you discover all this?"

Janet explained how she'd loaded a photo of the spray-painted crown into an online image search and how all the images that the search returned were from websites that talked about the symbol as the image of the Cleveland-based gang the Kings.

"What is a member of a Cleveland gang doing in Dennison?" Debbie asked.

"I don't know. I assume he moved here when he got out of prison, but I don't know why."

"Do you think he could have been the one who broke into the café?"

"I don't know, but I guess Ian and Deputy Vaughn must suspect that, given the message I saw on Ian's phone the other night."

"Yikes," Debbie said. "Well, we have to talk to him, obviously. I bet I can find his address online."

"You know I told Ian I would stay out of it."

"But you didn't promise *I* would," Debbie said. "Oh, that was easy. He lives outside of town, off Pleasant Valley Road. If I left now, I could get there and back before CSI comes on."

"You can't go talk to him by yourself." What was Debbie thinking? "It's dark outside! And he's a drug dealer and a gang member!"

"You're welcome to come with me."

"Debbie!"

"What? I'll say we're inviting people to church, and I'll leave him a brochure. That way it's all true, and what can he do? He can't get upset that someone is inviting him to church."

"He's obviously a rough character. He very much could!"

"It'll be fine."

Janet realized Debbie really was going to do this. And she also realized there was nothing she could do to stop her. "If you end up doing this crazy thing, you have to call me when you're back so I know you're safe."

"And to tell you what I find out."

"That too."

Debbie promised she would call, and Janet hung up. She felt unsettled. Debbie was walking into a potentially dangerous situation purposefully, and Janet felt...

Well, if she was honest, she had to admit she felt just the slightest bit jealous.

Janet was on edge as she watched Ian's favorite cop show with him that evening. Debbie finally texted during the last commercial break.

No one home. Will have to try again tomorrow.

"Anything interesting?" Ian used the remote to turn down the volume during the commercials and nodded toward the phone in her hand.

"Oh. No. Just Debbie."

Ian turned back to the screen. He was slumped against the pillows, and Janet leaned against him. Still commercials. Janet hesitated then decided she may as well ask.

"Any update today?"

"On the break-in?"

"Yes. Have you gotten any closer to solving it?"

"We're working on it, I promise, love. It takes time to follow up on every lead, but that doesn't mean we're not trying."

"I know."

She wanted to ask him about Bernard Sampson, but she didn't want to get Debbie—or herself—in trouble. Still, she could ask about the drawing on the wall.

"Ian? That crown that was spray-painted on the wall. That's a gang sign, isn't it?"

Ian sat up. "How did you know that?"

"Tiffany told me how to do a search online for an image," Janet said, then immediately regretted bringing Tiffany into it.

"That's right," Ian said. "It's a gang sign. And that's why I'm so adamant about you staying out of it. The people who might be involved with this are dangerous."

Janet bit her lip. She didn't want to push it, but she also wanted answers.

"Kim gave Debbie a copy of the security camera footage."

Ian took in a deep breath and let it out slowly. "In that case, you saw that the guy who was responsible is not someone you want to mess with."

"The video was so grainy and dark, it was hard to tell much of anything," Janet said.

"Exactly," Ian said.

"But it looked like something was written on the back of his sweatshirt. Were you able to enhance the image in any way to see what it said?"

"No," Ian said. "I know they show that kind of thing on TV, but CSI is not real life. In actuality, you can't 'enhance' a photo. You can only work with what's there, and the technology to do that is wildly expensive. It's certainly beyond the budget of our department."

Janet nodded. It wouldn't be right not to tell him that Debbie was already trying to get that done. "Debbie thinks she may know someone who might be able to help. A neighbor boy who is really great with videos."

"You know what I'm going to say, love."

"I know. You want us to stay out of it."

"This is a police matter."

"But Debbie got a copy of the video legitimately. And if we can find answers that you can't..."

Ian shook his head. "Good luck. There's no way a kid is going to be able to find something in that video we didn't. We're professionals. We'll find the guy who did this."

Ian's voice was strained. He was getting frustrated. Janet knew she shouldn't push it. But there was one more thing she needed to say.

"I'm becoming more and more convinced that the theft had to do with that old photo that was stolen."

"It's not related," Ian said. "There's no way a gang member has any interest in an old photo."

"So you do think it's Bernard Sampson who was behind the break-in?"

"I'm not even going to ask how you know his name," Ian said, shaking his head. "I think it's time to stop discussing this." He leaned forward and picked up the remote and pointedly turned up the volume.

Janet watched the figures on the screen moving around, but she wasn't really paying attention. She wasn't thinking about the photo, the break-in, mysterious car crashes, gangs, or any of it. She was thinking about her parents and their fifty years of marriage. About how she'd never seen her parents fight, in all that time. How she'd never really even known them to get frustrated with one another. As grateful as she was for their loving relationship and her stable home, she wondered if they'd ever fought when she wasn't around. Surely they must have gotten on one another's nerves from time to time and gotten short with one another.

No matter how much they sometimes disagreed, Janet loved Ian. And Ian was a good man, and a good police chief. Even if he didn't always take her theories seriously. Even if he dismissed her idea because she wasn't a professional. She leaned back and snuggled up against him, and he put his arm around her, and she knew that no matter what had happened with the break-in, Ian wouldn't stop looking for the thief until he found answers.

But then, neither would she.

CHAPTER FOURTEEN

F riday was always a busy day at the café, but Janet couldn't be happier to see the place full. Jaxon had done a great job rehanging the pictures. Ian came by on his lunch break and installed a new camera, so their security was back in place. Once they got the new print framed next week, the café would be as good as new.

Janet chatted with customers and made sandwiches as fast as she could. Finally, the café emptied out.

"You're distracted," Debbie said, sidling up to Janet just after she flipped the sign on the door to Closed. Paulette was wiping down the tabletops, and the lemony scent of soap filled the café.

"I am?"

"Don't worry. Nobody would notice but me. But you've got something on your mind."

"It's just this whole thing," Janet said, gesturing around. "The new theft. The old theft. The fact that they're clearly related, but I can't figure out how, nor can I get Ian to believe me."

"What would help you feel better about it?"

Janet sighed. "I don't know. I guess I want to prove the two thefts are connected. Maybe one of the people there when the cash was stolen has a connection to someone who's still in town today.

Someone who could have seen that photo on our wall and known what it meant."

"And how would you be able to establish a connection?"

"I guess I need to do more research into them." Janet sighed. "Which I guess means another trip to the library."

"Then why don't you go over there now," Debbie said.

"But we still have to clean up, and then we need to head to Columbus to meet with Norma."

"I'll clean up. You go to the library. I'll pick you up once I'm done here, and I'll drive us to Columbus."

"I can't leave you to do all the cleanup."

"I'll help," Paulette called. Janet hadn't realized she'd been listening.

"We've got it under control," Debbie said. "You go on over to the library, and I'll see you in a little bit."

"You're sure you don't mind?" This hardly seemed fair.

"I'll see you later!" Debbie called.

Janet grabbed her coat and bag and headed off. The library was just around the corner.

The sky was a crystal-clear blue, and the breeze rattled the last remaining leaves that stubbornly clung to the tree branches. It was cold, but the short walk was refreshing, and Janet's head was already feeling clearer by the time she stepped inside the library.

She didn't see Ellie at the circulation desk, but she did see Bob Stanton, an older man who worked part-time at the library in his retirement. Janet waved and made her way to the research terminals and logged in.

She pulled out the notebook where she'd jotted her fragmented thoughts. *Let's see.* She'd decided to start by researching Dorinda Meyer, Jamison Finnegan's girlfriend and one of the four people who had been close enough to the briefcase to have taken it. Her internet search last night hadn't yielded any answers, so instead she opened the vital records database, which contained marriage, birth, death, and property records for Tuscarawas County. She typed Dorinda's name in and found a birth record. Janet clicked on it and saw that Dorinda Jane Meyer was born in Dennison on January 17, 1922, to Mildred and Geoffrey Meyer. Well, that was great, but less than useful. She went back to the search page and expanded the parameters, opening up her search to include all kinds of records. This time when she typed Dorinda's name in, she found a marriage certificate.

Janet clicked on the image button and waited while it loaded. Aha. Apparently, Dorinda married an Anderson Andrew Abel, of Monroe, Louisiana, at Dennison City Hall on March 1, 1945. *He must have come up first in every alphabetical listing in his life*, she thought. She typed Anderson's name into the records search, but aside from the marriage certificate, no other results came up.

Well, it would make sense if Anderson and Dorinda left town after the wedding, since Gayle hadn't known what had happened to her. She supposed the next logical place to check would be Louisiana, in case they'd moved to Anderson's hometown.

Janet navigated to the town of Monroe's county clerk's page, but vital records weren't searchable from there. Well, she could always check the genealogies again. This time it didn't take long for her to find a family tree that mentioned Anderson. The family tree had been created by a distant cousin, and it showed that Anderson had married Dorinda and that... Oh, well, that explained the town-hall wedding and the quiet departure from Dennison. This genealogy showed that their first child, Karen, was born five months after the wedding, and that their second child, Mark, was born just a year later. And, according to this, Dorinda and Anderson both passed many years ago.

This was all well and good, but none of this told her whether Dorinda had stolen the money.

Janet decided to see what she could find out about Anderson's family. She clicked over to the newspaper archive database and set the parameters to search newspapers in Louisiana. Then she typed in the name *Anderson Abel* and hit return. An obituary popped up, giving her the same birth and death dates, and listing Monroe as the place where Abel and his family lived. So they *had* moved to Louisiana at some point.

After a bit more searching through the archives of the Monroe-based *News Star*, Janet found a piece that featured a number of families in the area who needed help for the holidays. The point of the article was to solicit donations to help needy families in town, and Janet saw that the Abel family had been among those families. WAR VETERAN SEEKS HELP KEEPING FAMILY WARM, the headline read. Dorinda and Anderson were asking for help with their heating bills, as Anderson was unable to work due to his injuries from the war. Dorinda worked at the local paper plant but didn't make enough to support her growing children, one who had special needs.

Well, that was tragic, Janet thought. She hoped they'd gotten the help they needed. She hoped they'd been happy. One thing was for sure though—they hadn't been rich. It seemed unlikely that Dorinda had taken the money and kept it for herself, given the way her life turned out. If Dorinda helped Jamison get his hands on that money, she hadn't gotten much of a cut herself.

Janet needed to learn more about the Finnegan family, about Jamison and Jasper, and especially about that car crash that Gayle had spoken of.

She went back to the *Evening Chronicle* archives and typed in the name *Wilbur Finnegan*. In addition to the stories about the promised donation and theft, which she'd already read, there was an article talking about a Holiday Homes tour in 1952. Wilbur and Evelyn Finnegan's home had been on the tour, among others in town, including a "grand Victorian" owned by Mayor Eric and Mildred Humphreys, a "Colonial beauty" owned by Alice Bradford, and "an arts-and-crafts gem" whose claim to fame seemed to be as the birthplace of automotive titan Guy Master.

Janet had known that the man who founded Master Motors was from Dennison, but she had long forgotten that fact. There was a Master Motors dealership outside of town, along with the other dealerships, but she had never heard of any connection to the Master family nor met anyone who was related to Guy Master. In any case, as fascinating as it was, the homes tour was not what she needed. She found several more articles that mentioned Wilbur in relation to his role as head of the Dennison Chamber of Commerce, a role which granted him ample opportunity to petition the city council for regulations that favored businesses in town. She made a note to ask Greg, the current president of the chamber of commerce, if he knew anything about Wilbur.

Nothing all that surprising, Janet thought. Next, she typed in *Jamison Finnegan* and was rewarded with a handful of mentions. Jamison had been a star on the football team of the local all-boys private school as well as something of a musical prodigy. There was no mention of Jamison in the paper during the war years, which she supposed was probably for the best, but after the war, he'd been... Oh, well now. He'd been arrested and charged with financial crimes and sentenced to five years in prison. That was in 1956. The article mentioned that Jamison had grown up in Dennison but moved with his family to Columbus in 1953.

Interesting. So Jamison had a demonstrated history of breaking the law to acquire wealth. And the Finnegan family left Dennison shortly after the war. She turned her attention to Jasper Finnegan. Janet typed in his name, looking for a mention of the car crash that Gayle had mentioned, but there was nothing. There was a human-interest piece about Jasper's collection of antique watches, but that was it. Janet supposed she shouldn't have been surprised that the crash—if it had happened—was hushed up so it never made the papers. But none of this did much more than paint a picture of a wealthy and not totally honest family.

She clicked back to the main search page and this time looked up their names in newspapers in Columbus. She found mentions of both sons' weddings, a few articles about the bank Wilbur started in that city, and Wilbur's obituary. She also found a few mentions of Norma, notably her induction into the local Chapter of the Daughters of the American Revolution, and an announcement of her marriage. Which was all very interesting but did not tell her anything about whether the Finnegan family had anything to do with the disappearance of the briefcase that day in 1944. From what Janet could tell, the family left town in 1953 and never come back. She wondered what prompted the move, but that wasn't recorded in the papers that she saw. If the family had any link tying them to Dennison today—and therefore to someone who could have seen the photo hanging in the café—she didn't uncover it.

So where did that leave her? Wilbur was close to the briefcase when it vanished, but by all accounts, the cannon that distracted everyone else sent him into a PTSD-induced panic attack that several people witnessed. It was unlikely he could have taken the money in the midst of that, with all eyes on him. Gayle said she hadn't taken the briefcase, and Janet believed her. And it certainly didn't seem as if she'd come into a life-changing amount of money. Jean Holcombe was still a question mark, but Gayle was adamant it couldn't have been her. Dorinda Meyer was dating Jamison Finnegan and had been close enough to the money to take it. She could have been in cahoots with him. But it appeared as if Dorinda hadn't gotten much money out of the deal, if that was the case. And Jamison and Dorinda hadn't ended up together, though she supposed there could have been all kinds of reasons they eventually split up. Still, it remained a distinct possibility that Jamison Finnegan had taken the cash before it could officially leave the family coffers.

Realistically, that was the only likely scenario. Given all that Janet had read about Jamison and his family, it seemed like the best explanation for what had happened. But the police were never able to pin the theft on Jamison. Why was that? How did he evade capture for something that should have been so easy to solve?

Janet was missing something. She didn't know what it was, but she couldn't help feeling like there was something she wasn't seeing.

Her phone chirped. She pulled it out and saw that she had a message from Debbie. I'M OUT FRONT.

BE RIGHT THERE, Janet texted back. She closed out of the terminal and headed toward the front of the library.

Ellie was now behind the circulation desk, and Bob was reshelving books in the children's area. "Have a great day!" Ellie called, and Janet waved and made her way outside, zipping her coat up against the bitter wind.

"Did you find anything?" Debbie asked as Janet strapped herself in.

"Not much," Janet admitted. "Mostly reasons to eliminate suspects, sadly."

"That's okay though," Debbie said. "There's nothing wrong with eliminating the people who didn't do it. That leaves space to find the ones who did."

"It seems like Jamison Finnegan must be the one behind it," Janet said. "I think he was working with Dorinda. That's the only scenario that makes sense to me."

"Then let's go see what Jamison's sister has to say about all this," Debbie said. "Maybe we'll finally find some answers."

CHAPTER FIFTEEN

he miles flew past, and Debbie, with her lead foot, got them to the address listed for the Finnegan Foundation a bit early. It was far off the beaten path, located down a dirt road several miles from the nearest town.

"What is this place?" Debbie asked as she pulled into the driveway, which was blocked by a black metal gate that matched the fence encircling the property.

"It looks like a horse farm," Janet said, gesturing to the horses in the pasture to the left of the driveway. She couldn't see the house, but a huge white barn and several paddocks were clearly visible beneath towering sycamore trees.

"It's the ritziest horse farm I've ever seen," Debbie said as Janet got out to type in the security code Norma had sent her. Once she'd punched it in, the gate swung open, and after Janet climbed back into the car, they drove slowly down a gravel driveway that led around the barn and under a grove of aspen and poplar trees before climbing a small rise and curving around to reveal the house. The wooden lodge-style home had huge windows and a wide porch with an overhang held up by wooden trusses.

"It looks like a resort," Debbie said.

"I guess this is her home." As gorgeous as it was, it did appear a bit out of place surrounded by flat Ohio farmland. It looked like it belonged in a western mountain town or at a ski resort. "She said to go to the front door and ring the bell."

Debbie parked in the circular driveway behind a Mercedes, and they walked up the steps. The door was taller than any Janet had ever seen. She rang the bell, and a moment later, they were greeted by a woman in black pants and a black shirt. She was probably in her midthirties, if Janet had to guess, and looked nothing like the photos she'd seen of Norma.

"We're here to see Norma Starr," Debbie said.

The woman nodded. "Come this way," she said with a slight accent. She led them into a room with a soaring wooden ceiling and a stone fireplace that took up most of the back wall. Navajo-style rugs warmed the polished wood floors, and caramel-colored leather couches were gathered in front of the fireplace. They followed her down a hallway that branched off to the right and into an office at the end. A woman with bobbed gray hair, a pink blazer, and thick-rimmed glasses was staring at a computer screen. Janet recognized Norma from the pictures she'd seen online.

"Hello," Norma said, looking them up and down. It felt as though she was sizing them up, and by the way she was frowning, Janet got the impression they had failed some sort of test. "You must be Janet and Debbie. How can I help you?"

She hadn't offered them a seat, but Janet stepped forward and sat in one of the club chairs opposite the antique cherry desk. Debbie sat in the other. One wall was entirely lined with shelves filled with leather-bound books, and two other walls contained framed photos and newspaper clippings that spoke about the work of the Finnegan Foundation. A wall of picture windows behind Norma revealed a view of the sprawling grounds.

"Thank you for meeting with us," Janet said. "Like I said in my email, we're from Dennison, and we're interested in learning more about your family's history in town."

"My father started his first bank in Dennison," Norma said. "He's a huge part of the reason that town is even on the map."

Janet knew this wasn't true, and she didn't appreciate the woman's haughty tone, but she forced herself to keep smiling anyway.

"We understand that he was a very important figure in town during the Second World War," Debbie said.

"He kept that town afloat," Norma said. "It was his generosity during that troubling time, and his insistence on helping the less fortunate, that was the genesis for the Finnegan Foundation in the first place."

Not only did this contradict everything Janet had heard, she also bristled at the way Norma kept referring to Dennison as "that town."

"We're specifically interested in finding out more about a donation your father made to the hospital," Janet said. "It was a cash donation, and unfortunately the briefcase containing the money went missing before it was able to be handed over."

"I know the donation you mean," Norma said. "Dad never got over it. That's actually the day he knew he had to get out of that town."

There it was again. *That town.* "How so?" Janet tried to keep her expression even.

"When the money vanished, from right under his nose, that was when he knew the people there would never appreciate what he did for them. That night, he started making plans for the foundation. It was many years before he would actually establish it, but that was when he made the decision."

"Did your father ever tell you what he thought happened to the money?" Janet asked.

"It was one of those girls. It had to be—they were the only ones around it. And the police never bothered to find out which one of them it was."

"From what I understand, your father was also within arm's reach of the briefcase," Debbie said.

Norma lifted an eyebrow. "What are you insinuating? That my father stole his own money?"

"We're just trying to understand what might have happened and what he might have seen," Janet said.

"Well, he didn't see himself—or anyone else—take it. And he didn't take the money back either. From what I understand, when the money was taken, he was having one of his episodes because of that idiot band director and his ridiculous cannon. When Dad had one of his episodes, it was a full-body experience. He was not in any state to be stealing his own money back, even if he wanted to."

It sounded as though Wilbur had experienced these "episodes" throughout his life. That made Norma's account of them somewhat convincing.

"We heard a rumor that one of your brothers, Jamison, was dating one of the women in the photo," Janet said. "Dorinda Meyer."

Norma shrugged. "It's possible. My brothers were always surrounded by admiring women."

Because they were the only men who hadn't joined up to fight, Janet had to restrain herself from saying.

"Do you know anything about Dorinda?" Debbie asked.

Norma shook her head. "I know nothing about her. If it's true, Jamison never mentioned her to me. I was just a child at the time, so I wasn't privy to the details of my brothers' relationships."

Janet thought about how to phrase her next question delicately. "If Dorinda was the one who took the money, is there any chance Jamison would have known?"

Norma cocked her head. "Are you suggesting that my brother helped steal my father's money?"

"We're not suggesting anything," Debbie said quickly. "We're just asking questions."

"You're barking up the wrong tree. Why would Jamison steal Dad's money for himself? My brothers were both set to inherit." She gave them a look that suggested she thought her argument was airtight. Janet suspected it would do no good to point out that if the money had, in fact, made it to the hospital, she and her brothers would have inherited ten thousand dollars less than otherwise. Stealing that money back meant it wouldn't be missing from their personal fortunes.

Debbie must have made the same calculation because, instead of pressing the point, she said, "Can you elaborate on why your father decided to make that donation in the first place?"

Norma sniffed. "Because he was generous. That was just how he was, always wanting to help."

Was that what Norma really thought? It was so far removed from what everyone else who remembered him had said. Or was that just what she told herself? Didn't most people have rose-colored glasses when it came to their parents? Especially when they had built a whole nonprofit on the idea of their generosity. Either that, or Norma was a master at denial.

"But was there something specific that motivated that particular donation?" Debbie tried again.

"He wanted to help the war effort," Norma said, looking at them like they were simple.

Janet decided to go for it. "We've heard rumors about a car accident involving one of your brothers shortly before the donation. The suggestion was that a young woman was hurt in the accident and the donation was made at the request of her family."

Norma didn't say anything for a moment. Her mouth was clamped tight, a muscle in her jaw working.

"Was there anything else you needed?" she finally said, pushing herself up.

They were being dismissed. They'd struck a nerve. Janet read this as evidence that the story was true.

"Yes, actually," Janet said. She stayed in her seat, and Debbie did the same. "We have one more question."

"Yes?" Norma's voice was strained. She stood, leaning over her desk, her hands on its surface.

"Do you have any family or friends who still live in Dennison, or who may have visited recently?"

"No," Norma said coolly. "No, we have no connection to that town whatsoever these days, for which I am immensely grateful. Now, Ingrid will see you out."

CHAPTER SIXTEEN

Well, that was an experience," Janet said as soon as they were back on the road. The car bumped over the dirt road, kicking up stones.

"She did not appear to appreciate some of our questions," Debbie said.

"No, it appeared she did not."

"But the car accident thing must be true, or she wouldn't have reacted that way," Debbie said.

"I agree," Janet said. "And I was trying to decide whether she honestly believed her father was generous, or if that was just a story she tells herself."

"It's neither here nor there, I suppose. It doesn't help us understand what happened to the briefcase."

"She seemed pretty sure her father couldn't have taken it." Janet adjusted the vent so warm air blew toward her.

"She couldn't conceive of the idea that he could have in any case," Debbie said. "But I actually think she's probably right. If he was having a panic attack—one of his 'episodes'—then it would have been hard for him to swipe it."

Janet took all this in. "Dorinda was always the more likely suspect anyway. I think she swiped the briefcase and handed it to Jamison, and he took the money."

"And from what you discovered, didn't share it with her?"

"He can't have shared much, based on what I know of her life," Janet said. "Or, at least, it didn't help her much if he did."

"Well, we learned one thing for sure," Debbie said as they finally made it back onto pavement.

"What's that?"

"Norma has no interest in 'that town.'" Debbie smiled. "I believe her when she says she hasn't come to Dennison in years and doesn't have any connection to it."

"I don't get it. She hasn't lived there since she was a kid. Why does she hate it so much?"

"There's no way a person can hate Dennison," Debbie said. "It's such a great little town."

"I can't argue with you there," Janet said.

For the next several miles Janet thought about the slideshow she was going to make for her parents. Dad had brought several photo albums by last night, and she planned to get working on it soon. She pondered how long fifty years really was. She was so lost in her thoughts that she didn't notice where they were. They'd made it back to Dennison, but Janet saw that they were in the north part of town and not near the café, where her car waited.

"Did you take a wrong turn?" she asked.

"I thought we'd make a quick stop."

Janet was puzzled. She was also tired at the end of a long week and looking forward to heading home, slipping into sweatpants, and relaxing for a bit.

"Where are we going?"

"To talk to someone," Debbie said. "Trust me." A minute later, she pulled up in front of a small blue house with an unpainted wooden porch and a sagging gutter.

"Wait." Janet read the name on the mailbox. SAMPSON. A gray sedan was parked in the driveway. "This is Bernard's house."

"You told me not to go alone," Debbie said. "And this way, you can tell Ian honestly that it wasn't your fault, that I dragged you here and you didn't know about it."

Janet considered for a moment. It wasn't like she had *chosen* to come here against Ian's wishes, right? Debbie hadn't really given her a choice.

"Let's go." Debbie climbed out of the car, and Janet didn't know what else to do but follow her. They crossed the small yard, walked up the steps, and knocked on the door. Janet heard movement inside, and she braced herself. This guy was a drug dealer and a gang member. She grasped her phone in her pocket, just in case. She heard locks turning, and then the door opened.

"Yes?"

Janet blinked. She didn't know who the man standing in front of them was. This was a middle-aged guy with neatly trimmed hair. His belly strained against his shirt, and he had warm brown eyes and a smile.

"We're looking for Bernard Sampson," Debbie said.

"That's me."

Janet blinked. This was Bernard? She studied his face, searching for any trace of the man she'd seen in that mug shot. Could this be the same guy? He did have the same crooked nose, the same wide forehead…

"Hello," she said. "I'm Janet Shaw, and this is my friend Debbie Albright." Janet thrust her hand forward. He shook it uncertainly. "We were hoping to talk to you about your whereabouts on Monday night."

"Are you with the cops?" He looked from Janet to Debbie and back again. Janet wanted to laugh. They were middle-aged women. She wore a sweatshirt that said BAKING IS MY SUPERPOWER. He couldn't really think they were cops, could he? "I spoke to the police chief yesterday."

So Ian had been there. Good.

"We're not with the police," Debbie said. "Well, she is"—she jerked a thumb toward Janet—"but not like that. We own the Whistle Stop Café."

Bernard's brow wrinkled. "You're here about the break-in?"

"That's right." Debbie nodded.

"Well, you might as well come in," Bernard said. "Like I told the police, I have nothing to hide."

He stepped back and let them enter the house ahead of him.

"Thank you," Janet said, stepping in behind Debbie.

He led them to a small living room with a worn recliner and a threadbare couch. "Look, I don't know who you are," he said, "but if you're here asking me about the break-in at the café, then you know I was in prison and you know what for. So I'll tell you the same thing I told the cops who were here yesterday." He gestured toward the couch. "Why don't you two have a seat?"

Janet and Debbie sat down, and he took a seat in the recliner.

"I was living in Cleveland, and I got in with a bad crowd," he said. "My dad was out of the picture, my mom worked around the clock trying to feed us, and my cousin offered me a chance to make some money. I took it. I shouldn't have. Before I knew it, I was involved up to my neck in something I didn't understand."

"When did you join the Kings?" Janet asked.

"It's not like there's a moment when that happens," Bernard said. "It's more like a continuum."

"Around when?"

"Nine years ago, give or take?" He sighed. "Eight years since I got this." He pulled up his sleeve and showed them a tattoo of a crown, almost exactly like the one on the café wall.

Janet looked at Debbie and back again.

"Being in a gang… It's not glamourous like you see on TV."

Janet wanted to laugh. When did being in a gang look glamourous?

"I mostly dealt opioids. Oxycodone, hydrocodone, that kind of thing. Then fentanyl became the thing everyone wanted, so I was moving more of that."

"Fentanyl? Isn't that what so many people are overdosing on these days?" Debbie asked.

"Yes," Bernard said. "It's a hundred times more powerful than morphine, and yes, you hear stories in the news all the time these days about overdose deaths related to fentanyl. Back then, people didn't know about it as much, so it was more under the radar." He sighed again. "Look, I'm not saying I'm proud of what I did. I'm just being honest. I was dealing, and I was caught."

"And charged with possession with intent to distribute," Janet said.

"I went to prison," Bernard said. "And it was the absolute best thing that could have happened to me."

"Really?" Debbie cocked her head. She looked as confused as Janet felt.

"If I hadn't been sent to prison, I'd be dead, one way or another. I'd have either overdosed or gotten caught up in the violence." He nodded. "I was out of control, and I knew it, I just didn't know how to stop. In prison, I was introduced to someone who changed my life."

"Who was that?" Janet figured a guard or other inmate had made an impression on him.

"Jesus Christ."

"Oh." She could have kicked herself. Of course.

"When I was behind bars, there was nowhere to run, and I had to face my fears. I hit rock bottom, and Jesus was there. I found the Lord, and He gave me the strength to make some big changes in my life. I started to attend a Bible study, and I intend to walk with Jesus for the rest of my days. And, Lord willing, I'm done with drugs forever."

"That's incredible." Debbie's tone had changed. It was less confrontational, more awed.

"I led prayer groups, started volunteering in the library, got an education. I passed the GED test from behind bars," Bernard continued.

"Congratulations," Janet said. That was a huge accomplishment.

"God is good," Bernard said. "Long story short, God got ahold of me behind bars and turned my life around. I got out early, and I moved here to Dennison. I wanted to find a small town where no one knew me or my past and where I could serve God, and the Lord led me here."

Janet wanted to be skeptical—was he just spinning a tale to throw them off? A good conversion story could win over even the hardest heart, and she remembered how Debbie had seen straight through Alyssa, while she had fallen for her stories. But the change in Bernard from his mug shot to the man she saw in front of her was incredible. That couldn't be faked, could it? And now that she looked more closely, she saw that there was a cross on the mantel and a framed copy of "Footprints in the Sand" on a side table. A well-worn leather-bound Bible sat right next to it. If he was faking his faith, he had sure worked hard to plant evidence.

"So, your question was, where was I on Monday night?" Bernard asked.

Debbie and Janet nodded.

"I was at my small group until about nine," Bernard said. "And then after that, I was here. I live alone, so I don't suppose anyone can vouch for my whereabouts, but everyone in my small group can vouch for the fact that I was there." He smiled. "We were studying Paul's conversion on the road to Damascus."

Janet knew the passage from Acts. Saul, a Pharisee who made it his mission to persecute the early Christians, saw a blinding light and heard the voice of God, and he turned away from persecuting Christians to become one of the most influential members of the early church and author of much of the New Testament. The irony was not lost on her that Bernard had been studying one of the most pivotal conversion experiences recorded in the Bible the night of the break-in.

"I know I can't prove that I didn't do it," Bernard said. "And I know that for some reason, whoever did this painted a crown on the wall, which leads right to me. But I had nothing to do with it. I hope you'll believe me."

The funny thing was, Janet did. She believed that he was sincere when he talked about how his life had changed, how his heart had changed.

On the way back out to the car, she asked Debbie what she thought.

"Oh, I think he's telling the truth," Debbie conceded. "I believe him when he says Jesus changed his life. The evidence is written all over his face."

Janet nodded. "It's pretty incredible," she said.

"It is. And it's also annoying as all get-out," Debbie said, shaking her head. "Because if Bernard didn't break into our café, then who did?"

That evening, while Ian relaxed in front of the TV, Janet sat down at the kitchen table and spread out the photo albums she'd gotten from Dad as well as the box of pictures she'd taken as a child. Her laptop and phone held many more photos, most of them much more recent, but she'd get to those later. She opened her parents' wedding album and flipped through the familiar pages. She'd loved looking through these photos as a kid. There was something magical about seeing her parents so young and in love. Plus she'd always loved seeing what her grandparents and family friends had looked like in their younger days. She gazed lovingly at Mom's high-necked sheath dress with the lace sleeves and the wide lapels on Dad's suit. They were the height of mid-1970s chic.

Janet chose a formal wedding shot of Mom and Dad posed at the front of the church and used her phone to scan it. Then she turned the page and scanned another shot of them posed with the bridal party and then one of them with both sets of parents. She also found a shot of Mom and Dad on their honeymoon—they'd gone to Chicago—and one from several years later, posed in front of the house she grew up in, Mom's belly swollen. Then there were pictures of Mom cradling a small bundle, and photos from right on through Janet's childhood—first day of kindergarten, elementary school concerts, middle school graduation. Janet enjoyed seeing the old photos and reliving the biggest moments in her parents' lives—and in her life.

She soon made it through all the albums Dad had brought over. She probably had way too many photos already, but it was so hard to choose. She decided to try to focus on the ones of just Mom and Dad together instead of shots with other family members included, but even then, there were plenty. She'd see how many she ended up with and then pare the choices down as necessary.

"How's it coming?" Ian came into the kitchen.

"It's good. I'm finding way more than I need, but I think Mom and Dad are going to like it."

"I'm glad." Ian walked over to the cookie jar and took out two chocolate chip cookies. He put them on a plate and poured himself a glass of milk. "The show will be over soon, and then I'll be ready to head up to bed."

"Sounds good." Janet felt a pang of guilt for not mentioning the visit to Bernard's house, but she pushed it down. "I'll go up when you do." When Ian returned to the living room, carrying his bedtime snack, she opened her laptop and began sorting through the earliest photos she could find on it. Oh wow. There were some on here from back when she and Ian were dating. That was when digital cameras were all the rage, before they were replaced by phones. She found some photos of Ian meeting her parents for the first time, shots from their rehearsal dinner, and some from their wedding day. She copied pictures featuring her mom and dad, gathering them into a file on her desktop, and then moved on. She found a treasure trove of pictures from a week they'd all spent at a cabin on a nearby lake one summer when Tiffany was small. There were tons of shots of Mom and Dad together, Mom reading picture books to Tiffany, Dad fishing...

As she scrolled through the photos, Janet realized once again one of the differences between digital images and old-school film shots—the abundance. She remembered her dad taking pictures at family gatherings when she was a child. He was very deliberate about framing the picture, making sure each person was lined up right and everyone was looking at the camera. Rolls of film contained a limited number of shots, and film was expensive to develop and print. But with the advent of digital photography, that limitation was gone. People could take as many pictures as they wanted, and that meant they could take ten variations of the same group photo, or the same sunset, or the same first day of school photo. They could review all the shots of a single instance and see which one they liked best.

Janet really liked the series of shots that showed a progression or told a story. There were the pictures she'd taken at a Father's Day dinner fifteen years ago. The first shot showed three-year-old Tiffany on Dad's lap, and the next showed her mouth open, talking. The half-dozen photos that followed showed Dad laughing and then setting her down on the ground. Seeing them all now, Janet remembered that Tiffany had tried to tell Dad her favorite joke, something about a frog, but she'd gotten it all wrong, and Dad found that funnier than if she'd gotten it right. Watching his reactions, they'd all been laughing. It was such a special time. Just one shot of that event wouldn't have told the whole story. It was interesting to see how a series of pictures could show things an individual photo couldn't.

Janet sat back, thinking about that observation. And then, suddenly, she had an idea.

CHAPTER SEVENTEEN

$\mathcal{S}$aturday mornings were always busy at the café, and Janet was groggy after spending much of the night tossing and turning, thinking about what she'd realized while sorting through the photos. Normally, she loved greeting their customers and meeting the tourists who came into town to see the museum. Today she was distracted and somehow managed to give Patricia's peppermint mocha to Harry and Harry's coffee to Patricia.

"Are you all right?" Debbie asked after she'd poured orange juice into a mug and served it to Jim Watson, the local newspaper publisher and regular patron of the café.

"I'm sorry," Janet said, shaking her head as she retrieved the mug. She really needed to get her head in the game. She turned to Debbie. "When things calm down, I need to tell you about an idea I had."

Debbie looked around the crowded café and laughed. "I predict it will calm down right around two o'clock."

Janet smiled, set the mug with orange juice aside, and poured coffee into a new mug. Two o'clock was when the café closed, and Debbie was right—it would probably be busy until then. Janet couldn't complain about the fact that they were busy. They had worked hard, and it was rewarding to see the café doing well. But today, all she wanted to do was get going.

Once the lunch rush cleared and Janet turned the sign on the door to Closed, Debbie said, "So what is it? What did you find?"

"I had an idea. Remember the photo that was with the original article about the theft in the *Evening Chronicle*?"

Debbie frowned. "Of course I do. It's the same photo that was stolen."

"But it's not." Janet took out her phone and pulled up the photo she'd taken of the article they'd seen at the museum. Debbie bent over. "It's *almost* the same image as the one we had printed and framed, but not quite. See?" She scrolled over to the photo of the picture that had been on their wall. "They're very similar shots, but see how Gayle's hand is in a different place here and Jean's hair is being blown back by the wind in this one?"

Debbie nodded as Janet scrolled between the photos, pointing out the differences between the shots.

"Okay, I see. They're two different shots from the same event," Debbie said. "The photo shoot of Wilbur's donation."

"That's right," Janet said. "So, I was wondering, what about the other photos that were taken that day? Presumably some of them were taken before these shots, and some after. Do any of them show what happened after the cannon went off?"

Debbie's mouth dropped open. "The photographer."

Janet nodded, relieved that Debbie saw what she was getting at. "He might have caught something on film. If we could just see the other photographs from that day—"

"But wait," Debbie said. "Gayle said he wasn't near the table when the cannon went off."

"You're right. And I've never heard the photographer floated as a suspect," Janet said. "Everything I've read says the only four people who were nearby were the canteen girls and Wilbur. But that doesn't mean there isn't something in one of the other photographs he took. If we could find the original series of photos he shot that day, maybe there would be some clue."

"But where would we find those?" Debbie let out a long sigh. "We're looking for unpublished photos from eighty years ago."

"I suppose we'd need to figure out who the photographer was," Janet said.

Debbie was quiet for a moment. "Or who hired him, maybe."

"What do you mean?"

"I don't know a lot about journalism, but don't most newspapers have photographers on staff?" Debbie asked.

"I think so."

"I'm just thinking, photography was incredibly expensive back then, right? It's not like now, when everyone has a video camera in their pocket. In 1944, it would have been rare to find an average person with a camera that could take photographs like this."

"I guess?" Janet wished she knew more about the history of photography.

"I think there's a chance the photographer would have been hired by the newspaper," Debbie said. "In which case, someone at the newspaper might be able to tell us more."

"But the *Evening Chronicle* went out of business in 1981."

"There have to be old records somewhere. Some way to look up things like who the photographer that day was."

Janet shrugged. "I don't know if there's a way, but it seems like our first logical step would be to see whether the museum has any information."

"Let's go."

"You're trying to find other versions of the same photo?" Kim wrinkled her brow a few minutes later. "Is something wrong with the version you have?" They stood in the main room of the museum, which was packed on this Saturday afternoon.

"Not at all." Janet shook her head. "We just noticed that the photo that was printed alongside the original article in the newspaper is slightly different from the photo we have." Janet showed Kim the same two photographs she'd shown Debbie, and she toggled between them, pointing out the differences. "We wondered if there were other shots from the same day somewhere."

"That's an interesting question." Kim pressed her lips together. "I don't remember seeing any, but let's go take a look."

"Are you okay to leave right now?" Debbie asked.

"It'll be okay," Kim said. "I have volunteers helping today. Let's go see what we can find."

They went back to the archive room, and Kim pulled out the files they'd seen before. She flipped through them quickly and then handed them to Janet. "Check here. I'll see if there's anything else."

A few minutes later, they had gone through all the drawers that could have contained more images from the photo shoot that day, but they hadn't found anything.

"We were guessing the photographer was hired by the newspaper," Janet said. "Do you have any clue where we might find the paper's records of something like that?"

"Oh goodness." Kim thought for a moment. "I mean, I guess you could talk to Jim Watson. I don't know if the *Evening Chronicle's* archives are with him, but he would be a good first place to check."

"That's a good idea."

They went back outside, and Debbie called Jim. Janet listened to Debbie's end of the conversation.

"Hi, Jim… Doing well, and you?… Glad to hear it… Yes, that's right."

Janet waited for Debbie to broach the topic of the call.

"I was wondering, do you have any idea what happened to the archives for the *Evening Chronicle*? Are they at the *Gazette*?… Oh, I see… Well, thanks anyway… I appreciate it… Have a great day."

Debbie hung up and turned to Janet. "He doesn't have them. He suggested we contact Maggie Gingerich. Her dad ran the *Evening Chronicle*."

Maggie was the principal at the local middle school. Janet had been on a soccer team with her daughter Anika when they were both in elementary school. Maggie had always been a warm, patient woman who brought the best snacks and juice boxes to the soccer games.

"Do you think she would still have any records from the paper?" Janet asked. "Didn't it close when we were toddlers?"

"Yes, I think so. But Jim says if anyone has the old archives, it would be her."

Janet smiled. "I guess our next step is to reach out to Maggie Gingerich."

"Looks like it."

CHAPTER EIGHTEEN

anet found an email address for Maggie Gingerich on the middle school's website and sent her a message asking if she had any records from the old newspaper her dad ran. She knew it was a long shot, and she spent the rest of Saturday evening working on the problem in the back of her mind. Even while she cooked dinner, cleaned up the kitchen, and got ready for bed, she couldn't stop wondering if those old photographs existed somewhere. But even if they did, she had no idea where to start looking.

Sunday dawned clear and cold. It was a pumpkin waffles kind of day, she decided, and she mixed up the batter. Once the waffle maker was hot, she poured batter into it and heated the syrup. While the waffles cooked, she gathered canned goods from the shelves to go along with the groceries she'd bought the day before. Today the church was collecting donations to give to the local shelter to help make Thanksgiving brighter for local families in need.

"What is that delicious smell?" Ian asked as he came downstairs.

"Pumpkin waffles." Janet kissed him and poured some coffee into a mug for him. "They're just about ready."

"Have I ever mentioned how much I love you?" Ian said.

"You can always say it again."

After Ian blessed the food, they ate, cleaned up, and managed to make it to church just as Pastor Nick Winston welcomed the congregation to worship. Janet tried to focus her mind on the service, but she was distracted, thinking about the break-in and the long-ago theft. Would they ever discover what happened to the money? Would they ever figure out who broke into the café?

Janet was almost glad when the alarm went off Monday morning. Now she could focus on baking instead of the break-in and the stolen picture. She drove to the café and started the coffee, and then she got to work. Her mind was soothed by the repetitive tasks—cut in the butter, mix the spices, fold in the eggs.

By the time Debbie got there, Janet felt a bit calmer.

"Have you heard from Maggie?" Debbie asked as soon as she stepped inside. With that question, Janet felt the precarious calm she'd enjoyed melt away. Still, it was gratifying that Debbie was wondering about the exact same thing Janet was.

"I haven't had a chance to check my email yet," Janet said. "Let's see if she's written back."

She poured herself a fresh cup of coffee, and while Debbie set up the register, Janet sat down at the laptop and opened her email. She almost gasped when she saw that she had gotten a response from Maggie, sent ten minutes ago. Of course, school employees were up early, just like bakers.

Janet,

How wonderful to hear from you. Anika is doing well, thanks for asking. She's still in North Carolina, and she and Howie are doing great. Their son, Chance, is very into baseball and spent part of the summer at a camp run by some major leaguers. I'll let her know you asked about her and hope you two can meet up next time she's home.

As for the old newspaper... My father was the biggest pack rat, I'm afraid. I have boxes and boxes of things that came out of the newspaper office. He could never bear to throw anything away, and I'm afraid I haven't had time to go through them myself since he passed. The boxes are all up in my attic. I don't have a clue what's in them, but if you wanted to come by and take a look, you're more than welcome to.

Say hello to your mom for me. I'd love to see her again sometime.

Best,

Maggie

"She has some old boxes from the newspaper in her attic," Janet said. "She says we're welcome to come take a look."

Debbie slid a still-warm pumpkin spice muffin onto a plate and sat down across from her.

"See if we can come by today," she said. "After work."

Janet nodded. School hours aligned with the hours of the café, so Maggie might be free that afternoon. She sent an email asking if today would work, and then she went back to the kitchen to check on the cinnamon rolls.

Janet didn't have a chance to read her email again until the lull between the breakfast rush and the lunch rush. She scanned the messages that had come in… Yes! There was one from Maggie. "She says we can come by after three thirty," she told Debbie. "She has to leave for a school concert at five, but we're welcome to look until then."

"Tell her we'll be there."

Janet used the next few quiet minutes to write out a shopping list based on the menu her father had set for the party that Saturday. He expected around thirty people, which meant they'd need three large tins of mac and cheese, three dozen servings of fried chicken, twenty pounds of potatoes…

She could have a grocery delivery set for Wednesday. That would give her enough time to start prepping beforehand but not enough time for the food to go bad.

After they got everything cleaned up, they drove to the address in Uhrichsville that Maggie had given them. Debbie pulled up in front of a beautiful Victorian home in the oldest part of town. The house was painted a deep sage green, the molding and delicate trim work were a bright white, and the house was surrounded by a wide lawn and tall trees. They parked in front of the house, made their way up the porch steps, and rang the doorbell.

"Hi there." Maggie opened the door and ushered them inside. "Janet, it's so good to see you. Debbie, it's been way too long." A formal living room with an ornate fireplace was to their right, and a set of stairs in deep polished mahogany rose to the second floor to the left. A long hallway, painted a rich shade of plum, led to the back of the house.

"Thank you so much for letting us come by," Janet said. "We'll try not to cause you too much trouble."

"You're free to poke around to your heart's content until I have to leave," Maggie said as she led them up the stairs, a thick runner absorbing the sound of their footsteps. "I'm so sorry it's not more organized. Like I told you, my dad, God bless him, couldn't throw anything away. And he loved that old newspaper. It was started by his grandfather, and he kept it alive for as long as he could. It broke his heart when he had to close it down."

"It must have been so hard for him." Janet couldn't imagine closing the café, and they'd only just opened it six months ago. She couldn't begin to comprehend what it would have meant to Maggie's dad to have to bring an end to the business that had been in his family for generations.

"It just wasn't financially feasible any longer, sadly. He took on a lot of debt trying to keep it alive, but he was about to lose the building. Finally, when he wanted to mortgage this house to keep it going, Mom convinced him he had to call it quits."

"Is this the house you grew up in, then?" Janet asked.

"Yes. It's a creaky old place, but I love it."

"It's beautiful."

"Thank you. My parents took good care of it." They reached the top of the stairs and turned down a hallway. "But as you'll see, having a house that's been passed down through the generations means you have generations' worth of junk in the attic." She opened a door, and another set of stairs appeared, this one far narrower and less grand than the first. Maggie flipped on a light switch and started up. Janet could smell the dust as soon as she followed behind her.

"Wow." At the stop of the stairs was a big open room under the steeply pitched roof. Furniture and boxes were piled everywhere.

"Don't say I didn't warn you." Maggie laughed. "Now, I think all the stuff Dad brought over from the newspaper office is in this corner." She led them around several pieces of furniture under dust covers and a rack of clothes covered in plastic. Then they squeezed past a stack of boxes labeled KIDS ROOMS, MEDICAL + DENTAL FILES, and DENISE'S WEDDING DRESS. Janet didn't know how Maggie could find anything in this place, but they wound past bookcases and trunks and ended up in a far corner.

"Here they are," Maggie said, indicating a group of boxes labeled NEWSPAPER. There were eight or ten of them, stacked in haphazard piles. "I couldn't tell you what's in them, but you're welcome to look around."

"Thank you." Janet hoped there was some system or organization within the boxes themselves. "We really appreciate it."

"I'll leave you to it, and I'll be just downstairs if you need anything."

After Maggie left, Debbie asked, "Where should we start?"

"Might as well start at the top." Janet reached for the box in front of her. "I'll take this one, you take that one?"

"Sounds good."

Janet opened the box and pulled out stacks of newsprint. She scanned the masthead of the issue on top. "Wow. These are old editions. This one is from 1965."

"Shouldn't those be in a library or museum somewhere?" Debbie had opened another box and taken out two clothbound volumes of what looked like ledger books.

"You would think." Janet shook her head. She tried not to let herself get distracted by the headlines she was seeing. She pulled out old issues by the armful and set them aside. As interesting as they were, old issues weren't what they needed. When she'd emptied the whole box and seen all there was, she returned the papers to the box and set it aside. Then she opened the next box in the stack. She quickly deduced that it was more back issues, so she was able to move through that one quickly.

"These are from a box labeled 'file cabinet,'" Debbie said, pulling out stacks of file folders. She opened one. "Look, here's a handwritten note from Mayor Buddy Pete. Do you remember Buddy?"

"Of course." Buddy Pete had been a larger-than-life figure in town when they were growing up, present at every public gathering and involved in every cause.

"There's all kinds of stuff in here. Business cards, check stubs.... And some of it is from Maggie's grandfather's era."

"Is any of it related to finding our photos?"

"No," Debbie said with a sigh. She put the folders aside. "But it gives me hope that we might find what we're looking for. It seems Maggie's dad kept almost everything related to the paper over the years and when the paper closed he just threw it all into boxes."

"That's the impression I'm getting too."

The third box Janet opened contained stacks of old photographs—black and white, color, matte, glossy, and from every era, as far as she could tell. There were also boxes of photo paper, an old-school photo enlarger, and bottles of darkroom chemicals.

"Looks like I found the darkroom," Janet said. "We're getting closer."

"Let me help you," Debbie said, and together they flipped through hundreds of photos. There were shots from ribbon-cutting ceremonies, fairs, Fourth of July celebrations, and high school basketball games throughout the decades. There were even photographs of the train depot at various points throughout the years. Janet loved seeing the evolution of trains over the years, from clunky steam locomotives to sleek midcentury styles to modern streamlined bodies. But nothing, as far as she could tell, was related to the photo shoot they were looking for.

"Nothing here," Debbie said.

Janet set the photos and the equipment back inside and moved on to the next box. She opened it and saw that it contained dozens of three-ring binders filled with plastic sleeves. Each sleeve held twelve strips of photo negatives, six on the front and six on the back. "Oh wow."

"How many binders are there?" Debbie peered into the box.

"There must be thousands of negatives in here." It would take them forever to go through them all.

"Are any of them labeled?" Debbie pulled out one of the binders, clicked the rings open, and held a page of negatives up to the light. It was too dark in the attic to see the images, so she took out her phone and used the flashlight function to illuminate the photos.

Janet examined both sides of the binder for any indication of a date. She checked inside the front cover but didn't see anything. She started to look through the sleeves.

"Judging by the fashions in this one, this is from the seventies," Debbie said. "Looks like a city council meeting or something."

"Actually, wait," Janet said. "There's something written at the top of this page. 'Ralph DeVito,' it says." She held the sleeve up to the light and guessed that these photos of the town Christmas tree lighting celebration were from the 1950s or early '60s, judging by the shape of the cars in the background.

"Maybe that's the name of the photographer who took the photos." Debbie's brow was wrinkled.

"I don't know what else it would be," Janet said. She flipped through the sleeves carefully. "So far, the ones in this binder seem to be his."

"Do any of them look like they're from the forties?" Debbie asked.

"No. From what I can tell, everything in this binder is from around the sixties."

"So hopefully, they're organized," Debbie said.

"Let's focus on finding a binder with photos from the forties then," Janet said. She set the binder aside and moved on to the next one. These negatives were in color, and the big hair and the clothes in the first photo she examined—a woman holding some kind of trophy—dated them to the early eighties.

"Hold up. This looks like it could be right," Debbie said, holding a sleeve up to the light. "This is a Packard from the early 1940s."

Janet leaned in and tried to see the image. "How do you know that?"

"My dad loves old cars." She shrugged. "I got dragged to a lot of car shows growing up."

"Well done." Janet scanned the other images in the sheet Debbie held up. They were so tiny, it was hard to tell anything about them.

"Do you think that's Wilbur's car?" Debbie asked.

"It could be. Harry said he drove a Packard."

"I doubt anyone else would have had a car like this around here back then," Debbie said.

"Is that a different car?" Janet pointed to the next row of images.

"Yeah. That's a Chrysler of some kind. I'm not sure what year."

"I wonder whose that was."

"No clue. But it sure seems like this photographer liked cars. There's another one. A Cadillac."

Janet looked at the top of the sleeve. "'Guy Master.'"

Wait. That couldn't be right. Janet knew that name. "The car guy?"

"I guess?" Debbie frowned. "I mean, he was from here. Would he have been in Dennison at this time?"

"I don't know. When did he start Master Motors?"

Debbie shrugged. "I heard he grew up in Dennison, but I honestly never paid all that much attention to him."

"Me neither." Janet shook her head. "Was he ever a photographer?"

"Who knows?" Debbie said. "Maybe it's a different person."

"It's possible," Janet said. But after thinking it through for a minute, she said, "But how many people named Guy Master could there really have been who were from Dennison around that time?"

"Yeah," Debbie said. "It seems unlikely."

"But it also seems unlikely that Guy Master, head of Master Motors, was a small-town photographer who happened to take the picture that hung on the wall of the café."

Just then, Janet heard the sound of footsteps coming up the stairs. She had to bite her tongue to stifle her frustration.

"Did you have any luck?" Maggie asked.

"Kind of," was the most honest answer Janet could manage.

"We're not really sure," Debbie said.

"Well, I'm really sorry to have to stop your search, but I need to head out for the choir concert," Maggie said. "You're welcome to come back tomorrow. And tomorrow I don't have any obligations, so you can stay here all night if you need to."

"Thank you," Janet said. "We'll be back, for sure."

CHAPTER NINETEEN

When they returned to the café, Janet got into her car and headed home. Over dinner, Ian told her about his day and how he'd been called to respond to a theft at the liquor store out by the highway.

"Do you think it's related to the break-in at the café?" Janet asked, spearing a piece of sausage.

"Very doubtful," Ian said. "In this case, the perpetrator took everything in the cash register."

"Oh my goodness. Was everyone okay?"

"Yes, no one was hurt, thank goodness." Ian sighed. "But I need you to know that we'll have to put most of our resources into it this week."

Janet took a bite, and she thought about what Ian was saying and about what he was not saying.

"You're telling me no one will be working on our case, aren't you?"

"I'm not saying that," Ian said. "I'm just letting you know that there's going to be a lot of scrutiny on my department in the next few days, and there will be a lot of pressure to catch the thief quickly. But I'm not giving up on the break-in at the café. Far from it."

"But in the grand scheme of things, the liquor store theft is more important."

"It's not more important, Janet. Not to me. But we have to prioritize the liquor store theft. I can't tell you why. You'll just have to trust me on this."

Janet decided not to press him, though she wanted to. She heard his message loud and clear. But that didn't mean she was happy about it. Why was a theft at a liquor store more important than a break-in at the café?

After dinner, Ian had to go to church for a meeting, and Janet cleaned up and decided she might spend some time with a good book to see if it would help her wind down. But just as she set the kettle on to make a cup of herbal tea, her phone rang. She picked it up and saw it was Debbie calling.

"Hey there," Janet said.

"Guess what I found."

"I have no idea. What?"

"Well, I went by the library on the way home. I dug around a bit, and I found a book about the golden age of automobiles."

"I had no idea there was such a thing as the golden age of automobiles."

"Sure. The 1950s. The cars in the fifties really were beautiful."

"I didn't know you knew this much about cars."

"You don't have to know a lot about cars to appreciate good design. Anyway, there's the other reason the 1950s were big years for automobiles."

"The interstate?"

"Well, yes, that too. The interstate killed the railroad, which was not great for Dennison, obviously. But that's not my point. Another reason the 1950s were so great for cars was that during World

War II, all the automobile factories were turned into plants for making weapons and planes and things the military needed. But after the war, they started making cars again, and the industry just exploded."

"I'm guessing there's a connection to Guy Master in here somewhere?"

"Exactly. This book had a section about him, about how he grew up poor in a small rural town—"

"It's not like we're in the middle of nowhere!"

"Back then, Dennison and Uhrichsville weren't as big. And we're hardly a thriving metropolis even now. Which is exactly the way I like it. Anyway, the book talks about how Guy did lots of odd jobs growing up, including working as a photographer for the local newspaper."

"It says that?"

"It does. It also says he washed dishes, installed drywall, cleaned chimneys, and had a paper route."

"You can't say he didn't work hard."

"True. But the point is, it's probably the same guy."

"Ha."

"What?"

"You said it's the same guy. His name is Guy." After a pause, she said, "Never mind."

"According to the book, Master Motors started small. In fact, it wasn't actually a car company at first. In the beginning, Guy started it as a steel company in Cleveland."

"I bet steel was a good business to be in back then."

"And Cleveland was a good place to do it, with so much of the shipping being done from Lake Erie. Just when the car industry was exploding, steel was a good way to get rich. Or, in this case, to get your foot in the door to do what you really wanted to do."

"When did he start actually making cars?"

"He started the auto business in 1949, out of the same factory. The first Master Motors car, a Stardust X9, rolled off the production lines in early 1950. It was a huge hit, and the rest is history."

Janet took all this in. "So Guy Master, the titan of the auto industry, was also the photographer who took the picture that hung on the wall of our café."

"That was *stolen* from the wall of our café," Debbie added.

"That's amazing," Janet said.

"It really is. Who would ever have guessed?" Debbie was quiet for a moment.

"So...where does that get us?" Janet finally asked.

Debbie let out a sigh. "Honestly? I don't know."

Janet heard the defeat in her friend's voice. She was starting to feel the same way. She decided she should let Debbie know about the liquor store and what Ian had told her.

"So they're not going to investigate our break-in anymore?" Debbie asked.

"That's not what Ian said. He said this new case is more high-profile."

"Which means the police are going to be focused on that one," Debbie said. "Where do we stand on our list of suspects?"

"Well, there's Alyssa. Just because the video footage showed a man doesn't mean she wasn't behind it. She wants us out of business, she acted strange when we talked with her, and we found her looking inside the café that day. She's still for sure on the list."

"Right," Debbie said. "Then there's Bernard. But after talking with him… Honestly, I don't think he had anything to do with it."

"I believed him," Janet said. "His story about how God transformed his heart… He's either genuine, or he's a first-class actor."

"Let's put him on the back burner for now," Debbie said. "What about that guy Curtis? The one who works at the gas station?"

"It could be him, for sure," Janet said. She grabbed a notebook from the kitchen drawer and started making a list. "He recently got out of prison for a burglary that apparently had the same MO. And he has the same build as the guy in the security camera footage."

"So he's definitely still a suspect," Debbie said.

"I think he has to be."

"Do either of them have any connection to the missing money or any of the people in the photo?" Janet asked. "Any connection to the Finnegan family or Guy Masters? Any reason at all to care about that photo?"

"Not that we know of," Debbie said. "But that doesn't mean the answer is no."

And that meant there were still some avenues they needed to investigate.

"Have you heard back from Zack about the video enhancing yet?"

"Not yet," Debbie said. "I'll check in with him."

"In the meantime, we'll just have to keep digging." If their case was taking a back seat to the newer, more exciting liquor store case, and the police weren't investigating it anymore, Janet didn't see what harm could come from her and Debbie continuing to look for answers. Somebody had to, and it might as well be them.

CHAPTER TWENTY

Tuesday afternoon, Janet and Debbie locked up the café as quickly as they could at closing time to visit Maggie Gingerich's attic once again. This time Debbie brought a small light box she used for drawing projects, in the hopes that it would make it easier to see the negatives.

"I'm sorry you're stuck driving again," Janet said.

"Ian still hasn't looked at your car?" Debbie asked.

Janet shook her head.

"Well, he's been busy. And I don't mind driving."

"You two have everything you need?" Maggie asked a few minutes later as they got themselves settled in the familiar corner of the attic. "Can I get you anything?"

"No, thank you. You're so kind to let us inconvenience you again," Janet said.

"You're not inconveniencing me at all. I just wish I had a better setup for you."

"We'll be fine," Janet insisted.

Once Maggie started back downstairs, Debbie picked up the binder they'd looked at the day before. "How about I keep looking through this one, and you see if you can find others from that time period?" she suggested.

"Sure thing." Janet worked her way through the pages of the binders carefully. She found one that appeared as if it could have been from the forties, but then, it could also have been from the thirties or the fifties, honestly. It was so hard to tell. And the negatives were hard to make sense of. The images were so small, and the tones were inverted—light where they should be dark and dark where they should be light. It was impossible. This was going to take them forever. Janet looked at the names at the top of the sleeves, but she didn't find any taken by Guy Master.

She made it through the first binder. She still wasn't sure what years it contained, but she was sure the photos of the day the briefcase went missing weren't in it. Which meant she only had about a dozen more binders to go through. She hoisted the next one and started flipping through the pages slowly. Sixties? Bouffant hair, Eames chairs, Beatles bowl cuts... Definitely the sixties. Well, not the photos they were looking for. Guy Master was already running a successful company in Cleveland by that point.

She skimmed through the binder quickly and set it aside. She'd just picked up the next one when Debbie said, "I found it."

"What?" Janet leaned in as Debbie unsnapped the rings of the binder and held up a sheet of negatives. She placed it on the light box, and Janet saw the images more clearly.

"This one." Debbie pointed at a picture in the top row. "That's either the photo we had on the wall, or one very close to it, right?"

Janet almost whooped in triumph when she saw Guy Master's name at the top of the sleeve. She studied the negative. "It's definitely from that shoot."

"Here are a few taken before it," Debbie said, pointing at the others in the strip. "And down below..."

Janet scanned the strip. The negatives showed a sequence of photos of the same scene. "There are about ten where the girls are posing with the briefcase."

"Right," Debbie said. "And then it looks like he took a few more after they were officially done. Candid shots of the crowd. And then several of Mayor Humphreys, and a couple of Wilbur Finnegan. And then—oh wow."

Janet saw what had Debbie so excited. "He was back again." Guy had returned to his original position in front of the table, the canteen girls on the other side, the briefcase between them. The girls were turned away from the briefcase. Gayle chatted with a man Janet recognized as Jasper Finnegan, and Dorinda was talking to someone off camera. Wilbur Finnegan was visible in this shot too, talking to Mayor Humphreys.

"Gayle said the photographer wasn't anywhere near the briefcase after taking the posed pictures with the girls," Debbie said.

"She was wrong." Janet didn't think Gayle had intentionally led them astray. It seemed that nobody had realized that the photographer had returned to the table. If they had, he would have been considered a suspect all those years ago.

The next photo was very similar to the one before, but she could see more of Mayor Humphreys and Wilbur. *Why did Guy waste film on candid shots like these?* Janet wondered. But she was glad he had, because the images that followed told a story. There were a few images of everyone relaxed and chatting. Then there was a shot where suddenly everyone's head was turned toward something off camera. The last shot showed Wilbur crouched over, hands over his ears, his mouth open. A look of terror was clearly etched on his face. A puff of white smoke hung in the air in the distance.

"The cannon went off just before this," Janet said, tapping the plastic sleeve that held the negative. It was the last on the page.

"And everyone turned to see what happened," Debbie said. "Everyone except poor Wilbur."

"He was terrified," Janet said. "That's clear in this photo."

"You can't fake a reaction like that," Debbie said, her voice somber. "He was in no state to take the briefcase after that. It would have taken some time for him to calm down."

"I think you're right," Janet said. "What happens in the next photo?"

"That's the last in the sequence," Debbie said. "Which means that the briefcase disappeared just after this moment."

"The four known suspects are all visible in this shot," Janet said. "And none of them are reaching for the briefcase."

"In fact," Debbie said, "it seems like the only person who could have grabbed it is whoever took this photo."

Janet saw it at the same time Debbie said it. "You would think that the photographer would have wanted to get pictures of whatever had just happened. We now know it was a cannon and that no one was hurt. But they didn't know that at the time. Wouldn't Guy have wanted to take pictures of the aftermath of the cannon firing?"

"But instead, the photos end," Debbie said. She tapped the image that showed Wilbur's fear and the three girls. "This was the last photo he took that day."

"Do you think that means…?" Janet let her voice trail off.

"I mean, it's possible," Debbie said. "He was clearly there, within arm's reach of the briefcase."

"And the photos show that everyone else was completely distracted," Janet said. "Our four suspects—"

"Were looking away from the briefcase." Debbie took in a deep breath. "Which means…"

"Which means it's almost certain that Guy Master stopped taking pictures because he seized the moment," Janet said.

Debbie nodded. "I think we know who stole that briefcase full of money."

"But what did he do with it after that?" Janet asked.

"And who stole the photo of the event from the café?"

Janet shook her head. "That's what we need to find out next."

CHAPTER TWENTY-ONE

When did Guy Master move from Dennison to Pittsburgh to start his steel company?" Janet asked when they were back in Debbie's car, the incriminating set of negatives tucked in Janet's purse.

"In 1944," Debbie said. "The book said he incorporated his company December 31, 1944." She drove slowly through the historic streets of Uhrichsville. Bare tree limbs arched over them.

"So roughly a month and a half after Armistice Day," Janet said. "And after the money was stolen."

"Exactly." Debbie nodded. "Surely the police questioned him after the theft?"

"They must have," Janet said. "Harry said they talked to everybody who was there. But he must have evaded suspicion somehow, probably because no one realized he'd gotten close to the briefcase again. Maybe he only showed them a few of the photos he took that day. Without seeing the whole roll, they wouldn't know he had opportunity."

"So he grabbed the briefcase, lied to the police, and got away with it. And then he left town right away. Hopped a train or a bus for Cleveland and used the money to start his company."

"Whether he planned to get into steel or just wanted to hide, he moved to Cleveland shortly after that money went missing," Janet said. "He started his company and never looked back."

"We don't know that," Debbie said.

"He certainly never returned the money," Janet pointed out. "But he must still have some connection to the town or to someone who knows what happened."

Debbie nodded. "Someone saw that picture on the wall of the café and made sure it disappeared," she said. "Or... Oh, Janet, they didn't actually have to come to the café to know that the photo was hanging on the wall."

"What do you mean?"

"Grab that article from the *Plain Dealer* again." Debbie indicated the glove compartment with her chin. Janet took it out and unfolded the page, and she saw what Debbie meant.

"That photo is in the background of the picture that ran with the article," Janet said.

"That's what I just realized," Debbie said. "Which means that anyone who saw the article could have seen that photo."

"It's tiny though." Janet looked down at the article, which did indeed show the historic photo. "You think someone could have seen this picture, noticed that photo, and understood what it was?"

"I think it's a possibility," Debbie said. "And if that's the case, then we're not necessarily looking for someone in Dennison. Whoever is behind the break-in could have been someone in, say, well, Cleveland."

Janet thought it seemed unlikely, but not impossible. "We need to figure out who, if that's the case. It couldn't have been Guy, right?"

"No, he's long gone," Debbie said. "But someone else must know the true origins of the company. If we're right about this, then whoever it was knew that if people saw that photo, they might start asking questions about that day."

Janet nodded. "We were looking for some clue in the photo itself, but the clue wasn't visible in the picture. The clue was who *took* the photo. That photo is proof that Guy Master was there and close to the money. And the thief knew that if anyone did some digging into the other photos he took that day, they'd figure out what happened to the money."

"Just like we did," Debbie said. "So now we need to figure out who stole the photo and how they might be connected to the Master family."

"Exactly," Janet said. "Where are we going?" Debbie had taken a right turn toward the highway. Janet realized that once again Debbie wasn't headed for the café.

"I figured we would make a stop on the way."

"You've got to stop kidnapping me like this." Janet shifted in her seat. "Where are we going this time?"

"You just said we need to figure out who has a connection to the Master Family. I figured we'd go back and talk to Curtis and see what he can tell us."

"You're going to go in and ask him if he's related to Guy Master?"

"I thought I'd try to be a little more subtle than that."

"Why would he be working at a gas station if he was related to one of the richest families in Ohio?"

"There are all kinds of reasons. Maybe he's a black sheep. Maybe he's a distant relative. Maybe he was disowned."

"I suppose it can't hurt," Janet said, though a feeling of dread gripped her. After the way she'd left last time, she wasn't sure she wanted to face him again. She almost hoped he wouldn't be working today.

Still, she could see that Debbie had a point. Now that they had a pretty good idea who had taken the money all those years ago, they needed to find the connection to the break-in. And the best way to do that was to see if the suspects had any connection to Guy Master or his family.

Debbie pulled into the gas station and filled her tank, and then she parked in one of the spots in front of the convenience store.

"What's your plan here?" Janet asked. "Are you just going to walk in and ask if he's working for Master Motors?"

"Oh ye of little faith," Debbie said, grabbing her purse. "Don't worry, I have a foolproof plan. I just need you to tell me if he's working or not. I have no idea what this guy looks like."

"Okay." They walked into the store, and Janet saw Curtis behind the counter, watching a video on his phone. Based on the screams and gunfire coming from the tiny speakers, it sounded like an action movie of some kind. He looked up as they walked in, but his eyes showed no sign of recognition. He turned his attention back to his phone.

Janet nodded at Debbie, who smiled and then wandered the aisles, as if considering different brands of beef jerky and motor oil. Finally, she walked toward the slushy machine and filled a paper cup with the red frozen liquid. She popped a plastic lid on her cup, grabbed a straw that doubled as a spoon, and carried it to the counter.

"That all?" Curtis said.

"That's it," Debbie said, her voice overly chipper.

"Two seventy-five," Curtis said.

Debbie dug the money out of her purse, and she also pulled out one of the business cards they'd had made up for the café.

"Have you ever been to the Whistle Stop Café?" Debbie asked, sliding the card across the counter.

"No." Curtis shook his head. "Twenty-five cents is your change."

"It's a great little place in the old depot," Debbie said. "You know where that is?"

"I don't," Curtis said. He held out a quarter, waiting for Debbie to take it, but she wasn't obliging.

"Oh, surely you've seen it," Debbie said. "We own it, so I'm always telling people about it, trying to build up our customer base."

"Cool." He finally gave up and set the quarter down on the counter.

"Can I ask you a question about my friend's car?" Debbie had obviously decided to give up on the café and try a different angle.

"I don't know much about cars," Curtis said. "I just work in the convenience store."

"Oh, but surely you know more than we do," Debbie said.

"Maybe. What's the problem?" Curtis asked.

"The car is making a strange banging sound, and we don't know what it is."

"I can't tell you anything," Curtis said. "Without seeing your car or hearing the sound, there's really no way to know."

"I guess you're right." Debbie shook her head and faced Janet. "You'll just have to take it in to the mechanic, I guess."

Janet nodded, sure Debbie was making a larger point. But before she could respond, Debbie continued. "I've been thinking about getting a Master Maestro. They're supposed to be reliable. Do you know anything about Masters?"

"I know I can't afford them. But that's about it."

Janet stifled a laugh. That made two of them. Masters were in the same league as BMWs and Mercedes—in other words, way out of her price range.

"It's a nice car." Debbie took a sip of her drink. "I read that the guy who started Master Motors was from Dennison. Did you know that?"

"Nope." He didn't know, and didn't care to know, based on the look he gave them. "You need anything else?"

"I don't think so." Debbie took another sip of her slushy and headed out.

"That was your foolproof plan?" Janet couldn't help but tease her friend when they climbed back into the car. "To ask if he'd ever been to the café?"

"What? It was a good question." Debbie's phone dinged. She glanced at the screen and set it down before she put the car into gear.

"It just didn't really get us an answer, unfortunately," Janet said.

"No, nor did my equally genius plan to ask him about Master Motors. It was like talking to a brick wall," Debbie said. "He wasn't giving anything away."

"Maybe he genuinely doesn't know anything about the break-in," Janet said with a shrug.

Debbie pulled out of the parking lot. "Anyway, I can see why you wanted to get away from him before. He gives off a vibe that... I don't know. He just seems menacing."

"Like he would break you in half if he could."

"Exactly," Debbie said.

"Do you think he was playing dumb about the café?" Janet asked.

"I don't know. That interview yielded exactly nothing in the way of useful information. He does seem to have the right body type, but that's about all I can tell you."

"On the plus side, you got a slushy out of it."

"Ugh." Debbie made a face. "Were they always this sickly sweet?"

"I think that's kind of the idea," Janet said.

"I used to like them. Now it tastes like chemicals."

"Welcome to being an adult," Janet said. "Just wait until you try Pop-Tarts again. So what's next? Do you want to try talking to Alyssa again?"

"Yes," Debbie said. "Although I'm pretty sure her shop is closed by now. We'll have to try that another time. But don't worry. That text I just got? It was from Zack."

"The Lego kid?"

"The Lego kid. He says he's done with the video."

"Was he able to enhance it? Do you think we'll be able to see anything more about the guy in the footage?"

"I don't know," Debbie said, turning left. "Let's go find out."

CHAPTER TWENTY-TWO

On the way to Zack's house, Janet found his social media page and watched some of his videos on her phone. She saw that he shot his videos in front of huge bins of Legos, and in each video, he would take pieces from various sets and create something entirely new. In one video, he took a pirate ship set and added pieces from a space set and turned it into a pirate-themed spaceship. In another, he used pieces from a Ninjago set and fused them with a pink-and-purple cupcake shop and created something he called a Ninja cupcake café.

"Maybe we should try selling Ninja cupcakes," Debbie said.

"I don't even know what that means," Janet said.

"I don't either. But the videos he makes are kind of fun."

"Yeah, I mean, if you're into Legos and have a lot of time on your hands, I could see why you'd watch those," Janet said.

"He makes tens of thousands of dollars a year on his videos," Debbie said.

"What?" Janet couldn't believe it. "For putting Legos together?" She had put together more than her fair share of Lego sets over the years. And those sets were expensive. He was getting paid to do it?

"He doesn't just put Legos together. He's a 'content creator,' according to his mom."

"We went into the wrong line of work," Janet said.

"Or we were born at the wrong time."

"I guess this is the world these kids are growing up in," Janet said. "Like it or not."

Zack lived in a two-story colonial across the street from Debbie's craftsman-style bungalow. Janet followed Debbie to the front porch, and Debbie rang the doorbell. They heard it echo inside, and then a woman opened the door. Her curly hair framed her face, and she had a warm smile.

"Hi, Debbie. Come on in."

"Thank you. Susan, this is my friend Janet. Janet, this is Susan."

"It's nice to meet you." Janet held out her hand, and Susan shook it.

"Thank you so much for allowing us to ask Zack for his help," Debbie said.

"Are you kidding? Of course. He has all this video equipment. He might as well put it to good use."

"It seems like he's doing all right with his videos," Debbie said.

Susan laughed. "Yes, he has fun with those, and it's great he's building up a college fund. Now I'm glad he's able to do something that's truly helping someone." She gestured for them to follow her up the stairs. "Zack's got it all ready for you in his studio."

Debbie and Janet waited as Susan knocked on a door at the end of the hallway.

"Come in."

They stepped inside, and Janet saw that Zack had turned a bedroom into his workshop. There were bins of Legos along one wall, a tripod set up with a camera, and what looked like several professional lights. A desk on the far wall had a computer with two monitors perched on it.

"Hi, Ms. Albright." Zack stood up from the chair at the desk. He was tall and gangly, with glasses and an enthusiastic smile.

"Hi, Zack. This is my friend Janet Shaw."

"Nice to meet you, Ms. Shaw," he said.

"It's great to meet you, Zack. We really appreciate your help on this."

"Of course. Are you kidding me? If I can actually help solve a crime, that would be the coolest thing ever. Let me show you what I did."

"I'll leave you to it," Susan said, and she ducked out of the room.

Zack opened a window on his computer, and an image popped up on the screen. It was the same black-and-white image at the start of the video they'd seen, but it was clearer, and the shapes were more distinct.

"How did you make it so much better?" Janet asked.

"The program I use to edit my videos has really great enhancement tools," Zack said. "It can correct for all kinds of things—bad lighting, bad sound, you name it. It can even make your skin look smoother, make you thinner, whatever you want. Every content creator uses tools like this to make their videos high quality."

"Don't believe everything you see on screen, I guess," Janet said. She had no idea there was software to do all that. Why didn't the police department have access to equipment like this? "I take it the software is pretty expensive?"

"Not as much as you'd think," Zack said. "But I don't think most people would have thought to use this kind of software for something like this."

Janet nodded. If this worked, she might need to suggest that Ian hire Zack to help out in the future.

"What I did on this was play with the saturation and brighten the lighting as well as adjust the contrast."

"It looks a lot better," Debbie said.

"It's still not a great-quality video," Zack said. "There's only so much I could do, given what I had to start with. But I think you'll be happy with what I found."

"Let's see it then," Debbie said, leaning in. Zack clicked on the arrow, and the video began playing. Janet looked at the bottom of the screen and saw when the man came into view. She watched as he walked up to the café and peered inside the window.

"There." Zack froze the image at just the moment when the back of the man's sweatshirt was visible. "I had to really bump up the saturation and the contrast here, but you can see what it says."

Janet gasped. He was right. She could read the writing on the sweatshirt.

"'Delaney Auto Dealership.'" Debbie looked at Janet. "Isn't that the car dealership outside Uhrichsville?"

"It's one of them, I think," Janet said. There was that strip with several car dealerships along the road, and Janet was pretty sure Delaney's was one of them. "Everything keeps coming back to cars."

"Doesn't Delaney Auto Dealership sell Master Motors?" Debbie asked. "I think there's a big sign for Master Motors over their car lot."

"I have no idea. But I do know that I suddenly want to take a trip out to Delaney's and ask some questions."

"Hang on. Let's see what else the video shows," Debbie said.

Zack pressed play, and the video started running again. They watched as the man smashed the camera and then broke the window, reached inside, and unlocked the door. Then the lights flipped on. A few minutes later, he came out, the picture clutched under his arm. Zack froze the video on the image where he was in profile.

"You still can't see his face," Janet said.

"No, I can't change what's recorded. Just enhance what's there." Zack smiled.

"That's really helpful though," Debbie said. "We're so grateful for your help."

"Any time. I love doing this kind of stuff."

Janet asked for a copy of the enhanced video to show Ian, and Zack gladly sent her a link to the Dropbox folder where he'd stored it. Then they thanked him again, and they left.

"So do we race over there now?" Debbie asked as soon as they were outside the Abbot house.

Janet checked the time on her phone. It was nearly six.

"I can't right now," she said. "I have to go home and get dinner started. Besides, I think we should show the video to Ian and let the police investigate."

Debbie stuck out her bottom lip. "But you said he's distracted by the liquor store thing."

"Maybe this video will reinvigorate his enthusiasm for our case."

"Let's hope so." Janet could see her friend was disappointed.

"Besides, we should probably do some research before we just storm in there asking who broke into our café," Janet said.

"Good point," Debbie said.

"We should also probably figure out if there's a connection between the Delaney Auto Dealership and the Master family and whether or not that guy on the video is related to them."

"Okay, you make a fair point." Debbie still appeared disappointed, but she seemed resigned.

"I'll show Ian the video tonight. In the meantime, let's see if we can discover any connections between Delaney Motors and Guy Master."

CHAPTER TWENTY-THREE

*J*anet reluctantly went home and started on dinner—pork chops, roasted brussels sprouts, and fingerling potatoes. But Ian was late. He was usually home by now. She grabbed her phone and used the locator app to see where he was. According to the app, he was still at the station.

WHAT'S YOUR ETA? she texted him.

A moment later, just as the pork chops came out of the pan, her phone beeped.

GOING TO BE HOME LATE. GETTING CLOSE ON THIS CASE. DON'T WAIT UP.

Janet stared at the message. He wasn't coming home? How was she supposed to show him the enhanced video? And what about dinner? Why hadn't he bothered to tell her before she asked?

Janet tried not to let herself get frustrated. Ian was the chief of police. Of course he had to take this case seriously. He was helping to make their community safer.

But still. It was hard not to feel slighted. He hadn't even called, just dashed off a text. He could have at least done it sooner. He knew she would have dinner ready by this time.

She served herself a pork chop, a portion of brussels sprouts, and a scoop of potatoes, and sat down and ate her dinner while she

looked at her laptop. First, she pulled up the website for Delaney
Auto Dealership. It was a slick site, with pictures of several shiny
cars. All of them, she noticed, were made by Master Motors. She'd
never paid particular attention before, but Delaney must be a Master
dealership. That didn't prove anything, exactly, but it was a sign that
they were on the right path.

She spent some time looking at the About Us tab. Delaney Auto
Dealership was a family-run company. It was started in 1976 with a
commitment to excellent customer service and a determination to
sell the highest-quality cars at the lowest possible price. That was all
pretty generic. The general manager was a guy by the name of Frank
Gavin, and there was a photo of him below his name. He was bald,
with a long gray beard.

Janet studied his face. He looked vaguely familiar. Had she seen
him before? She couldn't say where, if she had. Was he related to
Guy Master?

She wanted to do some research to try to figure out who the guy
in the Delaney sweatshirt was, but aside from Frank Gavin, none of
the employees were listed on the dealership's website. Besides, her eyes
were starting to feel very heavy. It was early, but she might take advantage of Ian's absence and go to bed at a decent hour. Janet closed her
laptop and cleaned up the kitchen, setting aside a plate for Ian for when-
ever he came home. Then she grabbed her book and headed upstairs.

Wednesday was a cold, drizzly day. It was not quite cold enough for
snow—just cold enough for things to be wet and slippery. Bad

weather usually meant fewer customers, but that was okay with Janet, as today was also the day the groceries for the party were set to be delivered.

"My goodness," Debbie said, eyeing the huge boxes that the delivery driver carried into the café. "Where are we going to put all this?"

It was a great question. Their kitchen, while commercial grade, wasn't large, and their storage shelves and fridge were already fairly full. Just yesterday, they'd had their regular delivery with what they needed to run the café for the week.

"I'll do some rearranging as soon we're closed," Janet said.

"It's quiet today," Paulette said. "We can handle things out here if you want to get started figuring out what's what."

Janet gratefully accepted, and once she had the vegetables sorted from the dairy from the flour and baking soda and found a place for everything, she felt much better. Before she knew it, it was time to close up, and after they cleaned the café, Debbie waited for her, purse in hand.

"Ready to go car shopping?" Debbie smiled.

Janet laughed. "Which one of us is in the market today?"

"You are, obviously. Your car is making a weird sound, and you're checking out your options."

Janet picked up her purse and slung it over her shoulder. "In what world do my options include a Master?"

"You never know," Debbie said. "It doesn't hurt to take a look."

Janet followed Debbie to her car, and as they drove, she asked, "Were you able to find anything about the employees of the dealership?"

"I did some looking around on social media, and I found a few salespeople who had profiles posted, but none of them seemed right." She gestured toward the glove compartment. "The printouts are in there."

Janet opened the glove compartment and looked over the pages Debbie had printed out. The first one was a profile of a senior sales associate named Brent Dickinson. He was probably in his mid-forties and had a mop of graying brown hair and thick-rimmed glasses. She couldn't tell how tall he was in his profile, but he was slimmer than the guy in the video. Next was a profile of a finance manager named John Bauer. He had a swoop of blond hair that covered his forehead and the same kind of thick glasses as Brent. She could see his shoulders in the headshot, and he didn't seem to have the same thickset body that the guy in the video did. The third profile was Mary Deloitte, a customer service representative who didn't look older than twenty.

"I think you're right," Janet said. "These aren't promising. But what about Frank Gavin? He's the general manager, according to the site."

"Right. He's in the glove compartment too."

Debbie really had a world of wonders in there. Janet pulled out the next set of papers and saw an obituary of Guy Master that had been printed in the Cleveland *Plain Dealer*. "Is Frank mentioned here?"

"Keep reading."

Janet skimmed the piece until she got to the list of Master's survivors. His children were Drew Master, Erik Master, and Linda (Master) Gavin.

"Frank is Linda's—what? Son?" Janet guessed.

WHISTLE STOP CAFÉ MYSTERIES

"That's my assumption," Debbie said. "Drew runs the company now. Erik lives in Hong Kong and is some kind of finance guy. And Linda married and had three kids of her own before she passed away ten years ago."

"You did a lot of research last night."

"I was on a roll."

Janet felt bad that she had just gone to bed.

"It was fun," Debbie said, as if reading her mind. "You know I love this stuff."

"Well, I'm grateful you found it." She folded the printout back up. "So, the general manager of the dealership is Guy Master's... grandson?"

"I guess so. Or in his daughter's family somehow," Debbie confirmed.

"Are all Master dealerships owned by members of the family?" Janet asked.

"I can't imagine they are," Debbie said. "There have to be hundreds of them across the country. They can't all be run by family members. But at least some of them are, I guess."

"It's the family business," Janet said. She thought for a minute, trying to envision how this would play out. "So I guess we just go in and see if we spot anyone who looks like he could be our guy."

"And then we do a citizen's arrest on the spot, obviously." Debbie grinned. "Kidding. Then we'll see what happens."

They drove in silence for a few minutes. Then Janet said, "I've been thinking. If our thief actually was affiliated with Delaney Auto Dealership, why would he wear that sweatshirt to commit a crime? Wouldn't he realize that would make him easy to track down?"

"Maybe?" Debbie shrugged.

"Not only that, why would he steal just one picture?" Janet shook her head. "If he had stolen several pictures, we wouldn't have known which one he was really after. By only stealing one, he shone a spotlight on the exact photo we needed to pay attention to."

"You make excellent points. Maybe the thief should have talked to you before planning his break-in." Debbie gave her a half smile.

"My point is, I'm guessing the reason he wore the sweatshirt with the name of the dealership on it is the same reason he did such a bad job of planning the break-in."

"Which is…?"

"He's not a professional. He's not used to planning heists. This wasn't a well-thought-out and professionally executed theft. It was carried out by a careless amateur who wanted to make sure no one figured out what that photo was proof of. Someone who was willing to protect the Master family at all costs. Who desperately did not want it to come out how Guy Master got the seed money he used to start his automotive empire."

"It's probably someone who's benefitted from the empire personally," Debbie said. "Someone like a relative."

"That's what I'm thinking," Janet said. "Let's see if we can find someone like that."

They were at the stretch of road lined with dealerships. When they got to the tall Delaney Auto Dealership sign, Debbie pulled off the main road and into a small area marked Visitor Parking. On the side of the building was the Master Motors logo. She'd never noticed that before.

"Here goes nothing," Debbie said. She slung her purse over her shoulder and gestured for Janet to lead the way. Janet approached a glass-fronted building. Half of the building appeared to be the showroom, while the other half was a garage. Behind the building were rows and rows of shiny cars. They came to the door and stepped inside. The showroom had half a dozen cars parked along the windows at the front and a row of cubicles along the opposite wall. Janet scanned the room. Was anyone here the guy in the video? It was hard to say, considering they'd only seen the back of him, but she looked for a tall guy with a stocky build. There was a handful of people in the room, but she didn't see anyone who fit the bill. She noticed an opening to the service side of the building, but before they could head that way, a man greeted them.

"Hello, and welcome to Delaney. I'm Liam. What can I help you find today?" Liam had curly brown hair and was far too heavyset to be the man in the security camera footage.

"We're looking for—" Janet panicked. *Don't say a thief, don't say a thief.* "A car," she sputtered.

"In that case you've come to the right place," he said with a grin. "Which one of you is in the market today?"

"She has a car that's making weird noises," Debbie said smoothly. "I'm encouraging her to look at options should she decide to replace it." Janet noticed that Debbie was careful to phrase it so that she didn't say anything that wasn't true.

"I'm happy to help you find something you'll love," Liam said. "Now, are you thinking of a traditional sedan, or are you interested in a larger vehicle, something like a compact or full-size SUV?"

Janet didn't have a clue, but she knew she had to answer, so she said, "I have a sedan right now. I've never really considered anything else." *But it would be nice to have an SUV,* she thought. *To be able to load cakes or trays and not have to balance them awkwardly on the back seat.* "But I'd be interested in seeing something with more room."

"I'm sure we can find something for you." He gestured for them to follow him, and he led them to a white vehicle. "This is the X275. It's a compact SUV, and it's one of our bestselling models. As you can see, it's got lots of room for passengers and the back opens with the touch of a button"—he pressed a hidden button on the hatch, and the door rose silently—"to allow for lots of storage space."

"Wow." Janet could put several trays in there as well as cakes and all kinds of other things.

"The driving experience is also as smooth as they come. Why don't you take the driver's seat and I'll show you the features?"

Don't mind if I do, Janet thought, and she slid behind the wheel. The car had buttery leather seats, and the dashboard was beautifully designed. Debbie climbed into the back seat and began playing around with the temperature controls while Liam explained the safety features, including automatic braking and lane assist.

"I don't know. I'm not sure how I feel about a car that's a better driver than I am," Janet joked.

"It also has a state-of-the-art stereo system with a built-in music subscription, and connecting a phone is easy, so you can set up your own playlists."

"You could listen to something other than just the radio for a change," Debbie said from the back seat.

"This model reflects the standard package, but of course there are lots of upgrades you can opt for—extra safety features, entertainment packages, sports packages, winter packages—whatever you're looking for, we can provide."

It really is a nice car, Janet thought, running her hands along the smooth steering wheel. And it was so much more practical than her little sedan. Safer too.

"How much is this base model?" she asked.

It was a good thing she was sitting down when Liam told her the number. Janet hadn't realized cars could cost that much. She could almost buy a small house for that price.

"Well, this is a very nice car," she said, sliding out quickly. "But I'm not sure it's in my price range."

"We offer extensive financing options," Liam said, undaunted. "I could set you up with a member of our customer financing team, and we could—"

"Thank you, but I think we'd just like to look around for a bit," Debbie said. "To get a better sense of what the options are."

"Of course," he said. "You go ahead and check out the other models we have on display here. If you have any questions, please don't hesitate to ask me." Liam pulled a business card from his shirt pocket and held it out.

"We absolutely will." Debbie took the card and steered Janet away. "Let's look at this one, Janet."

Liam let them wander off, and when Janet followed Debbie to the next car in line, she realized that Debbie wasn't actually looking at the car. She was scanning the cubicles, presumably searching for someone with the same body type as their thief.

"Not him," Debbie said, nodding at a slight man with brown hair. She moved on to the next nearby car, a sporty full-size SUV. "Not her." The woman in the next cubicle wore a gray suit and was talking on her phone. "Not him." The man at the end of the row had long black hair tied back into a ponytail and a tall, skinny frame. "Our guy's not here."

"Maybe he's in the service area." Janet looked at the opening that led to the service side of the building.

"Let's try that," Debbie said. They walked back down the length of the showroom before entering the garage waiting area. Three customer service reps sat behind a high counter. The room was ringed with padded chairs, and two coffee tables were covered with magazines. A television mounted on the wall played a rerun of a home improvement show. Janet scanned the people at the counter, looking for anyone who might be the right person, but two were women, and the man at the end was much too large.

"Okay," Debbie said quietly. "Next we check the garage."

"How do we get there?" Janet asked.

She looked around. There was a door at one end of the room that said GARAGE. EMPLOYEES ONLY.

"I guess it's just through there," Debbie said. She started toward it.

"It says employees only," Janet protested.

"Let's see what happens."

Janet started to refuse, but Debbie walked straight to the door, pushed it open, and stepped right on through. No alarms went off, no lights flashed. No one even seemed to notice. Janet followed Debbie into the garage, where two cars were hoisted up on the lifts.

There was a man underneath each raised car, and one hunched over the hood of another one. All of them wore heavy hooded sweatshirts that said DELANEY AUTO DEALERSHIP.

"Bingo," Debbie said under her breath.

The man under the closest car—a black SUV—saw them and called out, "Can I help you?" He had gray hair and a wiry build. Not him.

"We're just looking around," Janet told him.

"I'm afraid there are no customers allowed in this area," he said.

Debbie nodded. "What are you all working on out here?"

"Ma'am, I'm afraid we really do need to ask you to leave." That was the guy working on the car on the ground. He straightened up, and Janet went on high alert. He had the right build, the right baggy jeans and work boots, and he also had a bandage on his wrist. This was him. This was their guy. Janet saw that Debbie knew it the same moment she did.

"Now that looks complicated." Debbie pretended she hadn't heard him. She walked over to the open hood of the sports car he was working on. "You must know a lot about fixing cars."

"Uh…" He was obviously struggling with how to respond.

"Debbie Albright." Debbie held out her hand for him to shake. "And this is my friend Janet Shaw."

"Hi." He still seemed stunned. The man who had spoken to them first walked through the door and disappeared into the building.

"What's your name?" Debbie asked.

"Brody Gavin." He pulled his sleeve down over the bandage on his wrist.

Gavin. Related to Frank, then. A member of the Master family.

"I'm afraid I need to ask you to leave."

Janet turned around and saw Frank Gavin approaching. The general manager of the dealership. She recognized his long beard at once.

"Customers aren't allowed in here," he said, and something in his voice made Janet tense up.

"I'm sorry," Debbie said, walking toward the door. "We'll just scoot right on out. So sorry to bother you all."

Janet was right behind her. Frank stood aside, holding the door open. He followed them through the service area to the sales floor.

"Thank you for all your help. This is a wonderful dealership," Debbie said, hustling toward the door to the parking lot.

"Liam was especially helpful. He's a great salesman," Janet added just before they both stepped outside and hurried to the car. Debbie didn't even wait until Janet was buckled in before she put the car in gear and pulled out of the parking lot.

"It was him," Janet said. "Brody Gavin is our guy."

"I thought so too," Debbie said. "It's him. It has to be. He broke in and made it look like a standard robbery, when the photo was the target all along. We solved it." Debbie sounded like she almost couldn't believe it. "Case closed."

Janet took a deep breath. "Let's go to the station and tell Ian right now."

CHAPTER TWENTY-FOUR

They pulled up in front of the police station a few minutes later and hurried into the brick building that housed the Dennison fire station, police station, and village offices. They walked quickly to the police department front desk, and Janet greeted Veronica, the receptionist from Queens, New York, who kept the officers in line. Ian always referred to Veronica as the first line of defense at the station.

"Hi, Veronica," Janet said as she started to walk past her desk. "We're here to see Ian."

"He's in a meeting right now." Veronica looked up at her through thick glasses. Her dark hair was threaded with white, and she wore dangly earrings.

"Oh." Janet wasn't used to being told she couldn't see her husband. "Well, we'll just wait in his office then."

"It could be a while," Veronica said. "Big department meeting."

Janet looked across the open floor plan into the conference room and saw that the glass-walled room was filled with uniformed police officers, Ian at the head of the table. "Do you know when they'll be done?"

"Tell you what. How about I text you as soon as he's available?"

Janet looked at Debbie. She didn't want to wait. She wanted to storm in there right now and tell Ian she'd solved the case and tell him where to send the officers to arrest Brody Gavin. Debbie shrugged, and Janet sighed. She supposed she couldn't just go in there and interrupt the meeting.

"I guess we can go get some coffee," Debbie said. Janet nodded, unsure what else to do. She followed Debbie back down the stairs and they walked to Drip, the little coffee shop next to the hardware store. They both got pumpkin spice lattes—not as good as what they made at the café, but not bad—and were about to walk to the bookstore to browse when Janet's phone buzzed. She pulled it out and saw that it was Veronica. "The meeting's over," Janet said. "Let's go."

Janet knew it was silly to feel slighted. The police department having a meeting didn't mean Ian wasn't paying attention to their case. But she couldn't help feeling the tiniest bit upset anyway. Like the wind had been taken out of their sails somehow. And of course the meeting hadn't been about the break-in at the café, she could guarantee that.

This time, Veronica waved them in as soon as they arrived. "He's in his office."

Janet and Debbie crossed the main floor, which was dotted with officers hunched over their desks, and into Ian's office.

Ian looked up as they walked in. "Hey, honey. Good afternoon, Debbie."

"Hi, Ian." Debbie waved.

"Now is not really a great time for a visit—"

"We're not here to visit." Janet fought to keep the frustration out of her voice as she took a seat. Debbie sat down next to her. "We're here because we know who broke into the café."

Ian's eyes widened. "You do?"

He didn't need to look so surprised. "We do. His name is Brody Gavin. He works at Delaney Auto Dealership. He's there today, if you want to go talk to him."

"And…" Ian raised his eyebrows. "Can you tell me why you think he's the perpetrator?"

"We got the security camera footage enhanced," Janet said.

"My neighbor did it," Debbie said.

Ian nodded, no doubt remembering that Janet had told him about Zack.

"He was able to sharpen the video so you can see the words on the back of the sweatshirt the thief is wearing," Debbie said.

Ian blinked. Janet could tell he was surprised but trying not to show it.

She fought to keep the irritation out of her voice. "I was planning to show it to you last night, but you came home too late."

"I'm sorry. I was working on this liquor store case. We're about to make an arrest, so things have been crazy."

"I emailed you a copy of the video as well." That might have come out a little colder than Janet intended.

Ian turned to his monitor and keyboard. "Here it is. I'll take a look at it ASAP."

"When you do, you'll see that he's got a sweatshirt from the auto dealership. We went there today, and we found him. The guy in the video works in the garage there, and it's definitely him."

"He's related to the Master Family. As in Guy Master," Debbie said.

Ian furrowed his brow. "Who?"

Janet realized that, since she hadn't talked to him last night, he didn't know this either. "We discovered that Guy Master, of Master

Motors, was a photographer for the *Evening Chronicle* back in the forties."

"What's that got to do with—"

"We found the negatives from the photo shoot that included the picture that was stolen. They were in the *Evening Chronicle's* archives and labeled with his name," Janet said. "And Debbie found out that he did, indeed, work as a photographer before he got into cars, so we know it's him."

As Janet was speaking, Debbie took the book she'd gotten from the library out of her tote bag and held it up.

"Looking at the negatives from the photo shoot, it's clear that Guy Master is the one who took that briefcase full of money," Janet said. She pulled the plastic page of negatives out of her purse and set it on the desk. "He took the money that was supposed to go to the hospital, and he skipped town and went to Cleveland and used the money to start a steel company, which eventually became a car company."

Ian was watching them, but he didn't seem impressed. Instead, he almost seemed to be... Why did he look amused?

"So you can close that old case," Debbie said. "We solved it."

"And we know that someone in the Master family saw the article in the *Plain Dealer*, and that's how they knew about the picture on our wall," Janet said. "The photo was in that picture."

Janet didn't know what she expected Ian's response to be, but she'd thought he'd do something besides stare at them.

"So that's it," she said. "You can go to the dealership and arrest Brody. He's there now."

"Hold on," Ian said. "Let's back things up."

"Sure." Janet nodded. "Ask us anything."

"Let's start with the dealership. You went there?"

"Don't worry, I didn't buy anything, though Debbie encouraged me to."

"I just thought she should look. That noise in her car could be anything."

"That noise, which you still haven't checked out, by the way." Janet raised her eyebrows at Ian.

Ian didn't take the bait. "You thought you figured out where the thief works, and you decided to go there and get in the middle of a police investigation because of what you saw on the security video?"

"Watch it for yourself. You'll see what we mean," Janet said. "You told me the police department didn't have the tools to enhance the video, so we found someone who did."

"And you think this guy from the dealership—you think he broke into the café, not to rob your cash register, but to steal an old photo from the wall?"

"A photo that contained a clue about who actually stole the ten thousand dollars that was supposed to go to the hospital in 1944."

Ian nodded, but Janet could tell from long experience that he was skeptical. "And you're saying that the café was broken into and this photo was stolen so that no one would find out that Master Motors, the multinational automobile corporation worth billions of dollars, was started with money stolen from the old train depot in Dennison."

When he said it that way, it did sound kind of far-fetched. But if he would just look at the evidence they'd collected, he would see it was true.

"I'm saying that if you listen to us, you can solve not only this break-in at the café, but also the robbery that's been unsolved for almost eighty years," Janet said. "Wouldn't it be good to finally hold someone accountable for that?"

"I'm afraid the statute of limitations on that theft has long since passed," Ian said. "We couldn't arrest anyone for that theft even if we wanted to."

Janet was flummoxed by this response. Even if it was technically true, didn't he want to get to the bottom of this? Right a wrong? Why was he acting like he was helpless, when they'd just given him everything he needed?

"Start with the video," she said. "Then look at the negatives. It will only take you a few minutes. It all checks out."

Ian nodded, but he didn't seem to register what they were saying.

"Boss?"

Janet turned and saw Deputy Vaughn in the doorway.

"We're ready."

Ian sighed and pushed himself up. "Janet, Debbie, I'll look into this, I promise. But right now, I have to go."

"You can't just leave," Janet said. Not now. Not when they'd laid out the case for who had broken into the café and why. He was supposed to go out and arrest Brody. Or at the very least he could have another officer do it.

"I'm afraid I have to," Ian said. "The reinforcements from the state are here. We're about to go arrest the suspect in the liquor store case."

"Right now?" Debbie looked as incredulous as Janet felt.

"I promise, I'll get to this as soon as I can," Ian said. He nodded at them and walked out.

Janet sat there for a moment, stunned.

They both waited as the activity in the main part of the station hushed, after the officers had all trooped out.

"Well," Debbie finally said, "if they won't do it, we'll just have to help things along ourselves."

CHAPTER TWENTY-FIVE

ow did you find Brody's address so quickly?" Janet asked as Debbie drove through the quiet country roads outside Uhrichsville. They had agreed they weren't going to interfere—they would just locate Brody so they could give Ian a live location, so he could arrest him.

"You can find anything online," Debbie said. "I did a search for him while you were in the bathroom."

Janet had only been in the restroom at the station a few minutes, trying to wipe away the evidence that she'd been unable to stifle her tears of frustration. "I wasn't in there that long."

"The internet." Debbie shrugged. "It's an amazing place. I also found his rap sheet."

"So Brody's been arrested?"

"Oh yes, many times. Drunk and disorderly, assault, armed robbery. All in Tuscarawas County, so he's a local."

"You don't think he's the one who stole from the liquor store, do you?" Janet could only imagine how mad Ian would be if they showed up at Brody's place while Ian was trying to arrest him. He'd be furious.

"I wouldn't put it past him, honestly, but no, I don't think so. When you went to the bathroom, I watched as the police cars all peeled out, and they were headed west. If they'd been going to Brody's place, they would have headed east."

"That's a relief."

"It's kind of too bad though. It would have made it easier to get the police to pay attention to him."

Janet laughed, but it was a sad laugh. "How do we know Brody will be home?"

"We don't," Debbie said. "But the dealership closed at six, and even if he was still at work, we can't exactly go back there. I'd say we're probably banned from that dealership for a while."

"I guess I won't be able to buy that SUV after all."

"It was a nice car," Debbie said. "You have to admit you liked it."

"I did like it. If I were rich, I might actually consider it. But until my ship comes in, I'm afraid I'm stuck with my little car, if Ian ever gets it fixed."

"Maybe it's time to just take it to a mechanic."

"Maybe it is."

They drove in silence for a moment. Janet watched as farmland rushed by, dark and gloomy in the gathering night.

"You know Ian would do anything for you, right?" Debbie finally said.

Janet sighed. "I know."

"He's just been busy. Busy trying to solve our mystery, for one."

"I know." Janet really didn't want to talk about this. But then, if she couldn't talk about what was going on in her life with Debbie, who could she talk to? "It's just that it doesn't feel like we're on the same page sometimes. Like when he puts this other case before ours, it's hard to feel like we're a team. Why is this other case more important?"

"I don't know," Debbie said. "But I know Ian, and I know there must be a reason."

Jane knew Debbie was right. And she knew she was being petty and selfish. But now that she was venting, she just needed to get it all out. "But I'm his wife," she said. "Doesn't he realize I might know what I'm talking about? Back there at the station I felt like he was just about to pat me on the head and say, 'There, there, you skip off and let the adults worry about this.'"

"Janet, this is Ian we're talking about," Debbie said. "You know he respects you and your opinions." She laughed. "You have to admit, it does sound crazy that someone in the megarich Master family is afraid that an eighty-year-old picture in a tiny café in some small town in Ohio is going to bring his whole operation down."

She was right. It was hard to hear, but she was right.

"He probably wishes he could tell you all about this other case and why there's so much pressure on him to solve it," Debbie said.

Janet nodded. "He probably does." Ian was wonderful and had always supported her, especially in previous cases. This time, he really did have his hands full. He wasn't just ignoring her out of spite.

They drove in silence for a few minutes longer, the low hum of the car the only sound. Finally, Debbie asked, "What is it?"

"I was thinking about my parents," Janet said. "About what it would be like to be married to someone for fifty years."

"It is something to celebrate," Debbie said.

"It is," Janet said. "It's just, I wonder how they got so lucky."

"What do you mean?"

"They have the perfect marriage. I never once heard my parents fight. I never worried that there were problems. My mom never felt like Dad chose work over her or that he didn't respect her."

Debbie didn't answer for a moment. Then, finally, she said, "I've never been married, so I'm probably the least qualified person in the world to speak about this. But I can guarantee it's not true that your parents never fought. They probably just made sure never to fight around you." She flipped on her blinker and slowed as they came to a stop sign. "You never really know what's going on inside a relationship unless you're in it. I do know that. But I also know that your parents made it to fifty years because they made a choice, every single day, to continue to love and serve and honor one another."

Debbie wasn't calling her out, exactly. She was too kind for that. But she was pointing out that Janet wasn't exactly loving and serving and honoring Ian right now.

"Ian loves you," Debbie said. "Maybe he doesn't always get it right. None of us do. But give him the benefit of the doubt. He's helped us many times on previous cases. Maybe he couldn't drop everything to arrest Brody the minute we asked him to. But he will look into it."

Janet supposed it probably was true. Ian would consider the evidence they had given him, just as soon as he could. Well, he'd watch the video. She'd taken the negatives back for now. He could have them when he was ready.

Debbie slowed down, squinting at the numbers on the mailboxes as they drove past. The houses were far apart out here, surrounded by acres of land. But they were getting closer.

"Do you think that means we shouldn't go find Brody ourselves after all?" Janet asked.

Debbie laughed. "Oh, no. I mean, sure, he'll look into it *eventually*. But we came all this way. We'd better go find Brody, don't you think?" She braked and pulled into a rutted dirt driveway. A low-slung house sat perched on a rise in front of them.

Janet smiled. "Just try to stop me."

CHAPTER TWENTY-SIX

They sat outside Brody's house for a while. A car was in the driveway, and lights were on inside.

"He's home," Janet said. "We can tell Ian where to find him."

But neither of them made a move to leave.

Finally, after twenty minutes or so, Debbie asked, "What if we just go knock on the door?"

"And do what?"

"See what he has to say."

"You think he might tell you if he broke into the café?"

"No, I wouldn't ask him about that. We already know he did. I meant about his family. About Guy Master."

"I don't know. I don't think that's a good idea."

Debbie sat in silence for a few minutes and then said, "What if I go? That way, Ian won't be upset at you."

"I really don't think you should—"

But Debbie was already climbing out of the car. Janet watched for a moment, trying to decide what to do. Then she jumped out and followed her friend up the walkway. Whatever crazy thing Debbie was about to do, Janet couldn't let her do it alone. She hoped Ian would understand.

When Brody answered the door, Janet could tell right away he wasn't happy. This was a bad idea. They should go now.

"Yeah?" He wore a stained white tank top and his work jeans, and Janet saw a tattoo on his forearm of the same crown he'd painted on the wall of the café. Just below it was a bandage, no doubt covering the cut he'd sustained in the process of breaking their glass.

"Brody Gavin?" Debbie said.

He narrowed his eyes. "You're the ones who were at the garage today."

"That's right," Debbie said.

"What do you want?"

"We want to know why you broke into our café."

What was Debbie doing? What happened to just seeing what he had to say about Guy Master?

"Debbie," Janet began. "I think we should—"

"I don't know what you're talking about," Brody said.

"I think you do." Debbie was undeterred. "But we don't think you did it on your own. We want to know who sent you to do it."

"Why?"

Was Brody admitting guilt? Janet suddenly wasn't in as much of a hurry to get off this porch. She tried to muster up some of Debbie's bravado.

"We know it was you who did it. We have video footage that confirms it," she said. "We just want to understand why."

"Someone must have had a reason," Debbie said. "No money was even stolen. So why bother?"

Brody didn't answer for a minute, and then he started to close the door. "I gotta go."

Janet put her hand on the door. "Why go to all that trouble and not even take any money?" she said.

Brody paused, and then he shook his head. "I don't know," he said. "It was just some dumb stupid picture. I have no idea why Uncle Drew wanted it. Dad paid me to get it, so I did."

Brody's eyes widened. He froze.

"Get out of here." Brody stepped back and slammed the door. From inside, Janet heard locks slide into place.

That was it then. That looked like all they were going to get from Brody.

But it was enough.

CHAPTER TWENTY-SEVEN

Who is Drew again?" Janet asked as soon as they were in the car.

"Drew Master." Debbie backed the car out of the driveway. "That's Guy's son. He runs Master Motors now."

"The head of Master Motors was the one who wanted our picture?"

"I guess." Debbie's headlights swept across the intersection, and she turned onto the country road. "Unless there's another Drew. But actually, it would make sense for him to be the one who wanted the photo, since he's the one with the most at stake if the story about how his company was really started gets out."

"And he lives in Cleveland," Janet said, realization dawning. "I'm sure he saw that article in the *Plain Dealer*."

"I think he must have." Debbie nodded.

Janet opened the glove compartment and pulled out the newspaper again. She had to turn the overhead light on to see it, but there it was. The recommendation, and next to it the photo of Janet and Debbie in the café. The photo of the young women posed around the briefcase was plainly evident in the background of the picture.

"If you know what you're looking at, it's very clear what that's a photo of," Debbie said.

"So let's assume that's how Drew knew about the photo," Janet said. "He sees it, and he wants it gone. He somehow gets his—what, great-nephew?"

"Something like that."

"He gets his relative Brody, who lives nearby and isn't the most law-abiding citizen, to break in and steal it."

"Not realizing that there are other copies of the photo in existence—"

"Not to mention the negatives—"

"And the hundred thousand copies of the *Plain Dealer* in people's living rooms." Debbie chuckled.

"I suppose he must know there's nothing he can do about those," Janet said, "and he just hopes no one pays any attention to a small, nondescript photo-in-a-photo in a grainy newspaper article."

"And he does all that because he doesn't want anyone putting that photo and the genesis of the Master Motor Company together," Debbie said.

"Which, ironically, we wouldn't have, if that particular photo hadn't gone missing." Janet shook her head. "Did you see his crown tattoo?"

"I did see that," Debbie said. "Do you think he was in the gang too?"

"Either that or he just wants to look tough," Janet said. "Who knows? But it does make me even more sure he's behind it."

"He's behind the break-in, but so is his father, who paid him to do it, and his great-uncle Drew, who ordered it."

"So we need to get Drew to admit what he's done," Janet said, voicing a thought that had been rolling around in her head.

"What?" Debbie turned away from the road to look at her.

"What Guy Master did was a crime, and it affected hundreds of people and their descendants. Think of all the soldiers who didn't get the treatment they needed because the hospital didn't get that money. Think of Gayle, Jean, and Dorinda, all living under a cloud of suspicion. Even poor Wilbur, who may not have had the best of intentions, but did lose the money he donated to help the hospital."

"And think of how that ten thousand dollars turned into millions for Guy Master," Debbie said. "That money allowed him to start his company, which made him wildly rich."

"It's not right," Janet said. "And now we're the only ones who know what really happened. Well, and the Master family. If we get Drew to admit what he's done, we can demand restitution. We can right this wrong."

Debbie grinned. "What, exactly, do you have in mind?"

Janet tried to stay up long enough to talk to Ian when he got home, but it was already after eleven, and she could see from the locator app on her phone that he was still at the station. She didn't know how long it would be until he got home. She hoped the arrest had gone well and they had the suspect in custody. She also hoped Ian would now be able to focus on the answers she was ready to give him.

When she got up in the morning, Ian was still snoring. As much as she wanted to wake him to tell him what she and Debbie had decided, she knew she shouldn't. He hadn't gotten in until after two—he needed to sleep. She got ready quietly and left a note for him on the kitchen table. *Please call me as soon as you can about Guy Master.*

Then she left for work, unsettled. She didn't know if the plan she and Debbie had decided on was a good idea or a terrible one. Hopefully Ian would call, and they could tell him what they knew, and they wouldn't have to go through with it.

But when ten o'clock came and went and she still hadn't heard from Ian, Janet started to get restless. She called home and no one answered, so she called the station, and Veronica told her Ian was busy and couldn't be disturbed.

"Can you tell him it's me?" Janet said. Surely he could be disturbed for his wife.

"I'm afraid he said not to disturb him unless the building was on fire," Veronica said. Then she whispered, "He's interrogating the suspect they arrested last night."

Janet was annoyed. Ian had caught the guy who took money from the liquor store. That guy wasn't going anywhere. Ian could put off interrogating him for a couple of hours if he wanted to. Now he needed to go get the guy who broke into the café—and listen to their case against Drew Master.

She didn't hear from Ian in the next few hours, and by the time they were ready to close up for the day, she had pretty much made up her mind.

"You sure you want to do this?" Debbie asked, locking the café door behind her.

"Let's stop by the station again and see if we can get Ian to listen to us," Janet said. "We'll try one last time."

Debbie led Janet to her car and drove the short distance through the small town. When they got to the police station front desk, Veronica shook her head.

"I'm sorry, Janet. He's still in there."

"How can he possibly still be interrogating the suspect?" Debbie asked.

"He's a stubborn one," Veronica said. "But Ian's not going to give up. He's a good cop. He's going for a confession."

Janet knew enough about Ian's work to understand that he only had circumstantial evidence against the suspect. He must have been arrested for probable cause, and Ian was hoping to make the charges stick by getting the guy to confess. If the case went to trial, he needed to make sure the criminal didn't get off because he didn't have enough evidence.

"He didn't wait to arrest him until he had irrefutable evidence?" Janet said.

"He was under a lot of pressure to make an arrest," Veronica said. "He got the guy, though. It's him. Ian will get him to confess."

Janet knew he would. She also knew that, as important as the news about Guy Master was, it would not be something Ian would stop interrogating a witness for. They were on their own. Again.

"Will you please let him know we came by?" Janet asked.

"As soon as he comes up for air, I'll let him know."

Janet turned to Debbie, who nodded and followed her down the stairs.

"What do you think?" Debbie asked.

"I think Ian is too busy to work on our case right now," Janet said. "And even if he was listening to us, he wouldn't be spending time worrying about an eighty-year-old briefcase theft, as he made clear yesterday." She took in a deep breath and let it out slowly. "I think that if we have any hope of getting answers and righting a wrong, we should get on the road to Cleveland."

CHAPTER TWENTY-EIGHT

*C*leveland was about an hour and a half from Dennison, but the drive felt much faster that day. As Debbie drove, Janet read up on Drew and his family and looked at photos of them all. They had Drew Master's address—the internet was the gift that kept on giving—and Janet insisted they would just talk to him. See what they could get him to admit. Let him know they were onto him. Then they would turn over what they knew to the police, and, if the police wouldn't listen, they would go to the media.

Janet had a slight bit of guilt about going against what Ian wanted, but she was also frustrated at how he hadn't acted on what she'd told him. She and Debbie had already gathered almost all the evidence in this case, and maybe if they just gathered the last bit, Ian would swoop in and make the arrest. He would look like a hero for solving two cases in such a short time—three, if you counted the historic theft.

"We won't make the police look bad," Debbie said. "We could just talk to a reporter at the paper and let them know what we found. I bet they would run with the story."

"I bet they would listen," Janet agreed. They rode in silence for a minute longer. "Do you think we should have called a reporter before we came up here? Maybe let them try to talk to Drew?"

Janet wasn't having second thoughts, exactly. She wanted to see this thing through, no matter how it played out. She just wondered if a reporter might have better luck getting actual answers from Drew.

"It's too late now," Debbie said. Did that mean she was having second thoughts too? Janet couldn't read her tone.

"What do we do if he won't talk to us?"

"Then I guess all we've lost is some gas," Debbie said. "And we could always go see Tiffany." She smiled. "Let's see how it goes. He may not even be home. Let's hope he is and that he'll talk to us."

Debbie followed the directions on her phone carefully, and the closer they got, the more nervous Janet became. A person couldn't just walk up to someone who might have security personnel keeping people from getting access to their boss.

But then she realized that they were also the only people who knew the terrible secret Drew and his family had clearly taken some extraordinary steps to try and keep hidden. They might be small-town café owners, but they'd managed to uncover the fact that Drew's father Guy was responsible for the theft of ten thousand dollars that was supposed to go to a hospital but instead had been used to start his business. They alone knew that the successful car company Drew ran had been built on lies and theft. If the secret got out, it would be disastrous for Master Motors. She and Debbie were a major threat to Drew and the company.

The address Debbie had found for Drew wasn't in downtown Cleveland itself but was located in Hunting Valley, a tiny suburb to the east of the city. As they got closer, Janet could see that the homes were large and stately, separated by big yards with mature trees and high fences. Lights burned inside the homes, making them look warm and snug against the gathering twilight.

"It should be just up there," Debbie said. They followed the directions on the screen and turned in to a gravel driveway blocked by a gate. "These rich people really love their gates, don't they?"

After this long drive, would they even be able to get past the barrier? Maybe this whole thing was a big wild goose chase.

Debbie stopped at the gate and rolled down her window. She reached out and pressed a button on a speaker. It buzzed.

"Yes?" The voice that answered was a woman's voice, and older. Bored.

"We're here to speak with Drew Master." Janet was impressed by how authoritative Debbie sounded.

"Who is this?"

"Debbie Albright and Janet Shaw." Debbie looked over at Janet, who shrugged. "We're from the Whistle Stop Café in Dennison, and I think he's definitely going to want to talk to us before we tell the press what we've uncovered about his father."

There was silence on the other end of the line. It lasted so long that Janet started think the woman had simply gone away, leaving them to figure out that they'd been dismissed. But just as Debbie reached out to press the button again, there was a buzz, and the gate rolled open.

"I guess we're in," Debbie said. After they drove through the gate, it closed behind them. Debbie drove down the long gravel driveway lined with large trees that stood stark and bare. The drive-way ended in a semicircle, with a parking area to one side. Debbie parked between two Masters, and Janet gazed up at the house. It was two stories with several gables and many chimneys. Black shutters stood out against the brick, and the home was lit up with footlights that showcased its stately old character as the darkness gathered.

Janet took a deep breath and took out her phone. She pulled up her voice memo app and tapped the red button.

"What are you doing?" Debbie asked.

"Recording," Janet said. "Whatever happens, I want proof."

"Good thinking," Debbie said, and did the same.

They walked together up the steps, and Janet rang the doorbell. It echoed inside, and the door opened to reveal a woman with shoulder-length white hair. She wore slacks and a turtleneck sweater—cashmere?—and gazed at them imperiously. Janet guessed this was Drew's wife, Gina.

"For some reason, Drew is willing to hear you out," she said. "Though I told him to just send you on your way."

"We're glad he's willing to speak with us," Debbie said.

Gina closed the door behind them and locked it, and then gestured to indicate they should follow her. She led them past a grand living room decorated in French country style, a kitchen with the same country aesthetic, and into a room that Janet guessed was originally a library but now was dominated by a large walnut desk. Bookshelves stuffed with old volumes lined the walls, and there was a small leather couch opposite the enormous desk. A gray-haired man sat behind the desk, and he looked up from a sleek monitor as they walked in. Drew. Janet recognized him from the picture she had seen online.

"Let me know if you need anything," Gina said to her husband. She closed the door behind herself as she walked out.

"So." Drew indicated they should sit on the couch. They sat, and Janet realized it was low enough that they had to look up at Drew and his huge desk. She supposed it was designed that way to make other people feel small.

"You mentioned you uncovered something about my father you intended to talk to the press about," Drew said. "His legacy is very important, as you no doubt understand. How much?"

"Excuse me?" Janet said.

"I get people like you coming around sometimes, threatening to trade rumors to the press in exchange for a quick payday. I used to fight it, but it's so exhausting and a waste of my time. I've found that it's usually best to just make the problem go away. So, how much do you want? A thousand?"

This was not going the way Janet had expected.

"A thousand?" Did he mean dollars? "You're offering us a thousand dollars to hush up what we know?" Janet couldn't be hearing this right.

"It's a fair offer. Five hundred for each of you. Buy yourselves something nice."

"Are you seriously trying to buy our silence?" Debbie looked as shocked as Janet felt.

"Like I said, it's easiest. I mean, of course, if you do decide to go to the press and share whatever unsubstantiated rumors you think you know, I'll slap you with a defamation case before the newspaper ink is dried, but lawyers are so costly, and the process can be so drawn out. Better to just take the money and run, right?"

Janet looked at Debbie, whose eyes were narrowed, her mouth open. "Are you serious?"

"Fifteen hundred then."

"We're not here for money," Janet said, trying to keep her voice even. "We're here because we want to know the truth. We know your father took advantage of an opportunity and ran off from the Dennison depot with a briefcase full of cash in 1944. We know he used the money—ten thousand dollars—to start his company. We know there is photographic evidence of the theft, and we know you know it too, because you saw the photograph hanging on the wall of our café in the picture in the Cleveland *Plain Dealer*."

"We also know that you saw that picture, recognized the historic photo for what it was—a clue that linked your father to the missing cash—and hired a relative in Dennison to break in and steal it." Debbie's chin was lifted, her voice strong. "We know that you wanted to make sure no one figured out what happened to that money."

"Two thousand dollars," Drew said, as if he hadn't heard them. "A thousand each. That's not a bad payday, is it?"

"We don't want money for ourselves," Janet said. "We want restitution."

"Restitution?" He laughed. "For what? My father did nothing wrong. The vile lies you're accusing him of are false, and I won't stand for you smearing his name like this." He started to push himself up.

"If they're lies, then why did you try so hard to make sure no one knew about the briefcase?" Debbie asked. "You sure went to a lot of trouble to get rid of that picture. Why would you do that if what we're saying isn't true?"

"You have no proof of anything," Drew said. "There is no way to prove my father took that money."

Janet thought about Ian, interrogating his witness. All he had was circumstantial evidence, and he was working to get a confession so he could make the charges stick. Janet channeled Ian as she answered Drew now.

"Maybe not," she said, "but we sure do have a lot of evidence that makes a really strong case. We have the negatives of all the photos your father took that day—not just the one that was displayed on the wall—and they make it clear he's the only one who could have taken the money. We know that he left town after the theft and started his company soon after. It paints a compelling story. I'm sure any journalist would be able to get a lot of attention for it."

"You don't have the negatives," Drew said, but suddenly his skin lightened by a shade. "They don't exist. We tried to find them years ago and were told they'd been destroyed when the paper closed."

"They were not destroyed," Janet said. "We have them." They were in her purse, but suddenly she wished she'd thought to take them out before they'd come. If Drew got his hands on them, they'd lose their leverage.

"Where are they?" Drew demanded.

"We might be willing to talk about where they are, but first let's circle back to the restitution conversation," Janet said. "Ten thousand dollars in 1944 would be worth about a hundred and seventy thousand today. There's nothing that can be done to help the people who would have been helped by that money in 1944 and the years since, but I wonder what the hospital could do with a donation of that size today."

"You're out of your mind," Drew said. "A donation of that size is out of the question."

"That's too bad," Debbie said. "Because once the story gets out about how the company really started, just think what it's going to do to the Master stock price. A donation of that size would probably seem like a good deal."

Janet wanted to pump her fist. It was a sucker punch, and it landed.

"Where are those negatives?" Drew stood and made his way around his mammoth desk. Janet looped her arm through the straps of her purse and held it to her chest. "You have them there, don't you?"

"You'll never get them unless you admit what happened and pay it back," Debbie said. Suddenly, Janet realized what a precarious position they were in. Locked inside his house. Behind a locked gate. No one knew they were here. A man coming toward them, a crazed look in his eyes. He wouldn't really hurt them, would he?

Somewhere out in the main part of the house, Janet heard raised voices, but in here, all she could focus on was making sure Drew didn't get her purse.

"Don't you dare touch me," she said, pushing back against the cushions as far as she could.

"Give me the negatives," Drew said, his voice an almost eerie monotone. "Hand them over now, and no one will get hurt."

"Threaten me one more time, and I'll call the police," Janet said.

"Good luck." Drew laughed. "We have private security around here. The regular police couldn't get inside the gate."

Was that true? Were they truly stuck here without any hope for help? Maybe she could call Ian. It would take him an hour and a half to get here though. Could she keep this man from getting the negatives for that long?

Again she heard the raised voices from somewhere in the house, but the sounds were muffled, and she could barely hear them above the pounding of her heart.

"Just hand them over," Drew said. "And then you can go. All of this will be forgotten."

"No, it won't," Debbie said. "Do you honestly think we won't tell everyone what we know, now that you've admitted it?"

What was she doing? Did Debbie truly not see how much danger they were in? Why was she goading him?

The raised voices got closer—someone shouted in the hallway. What was going on? Was that the private security force?

"Give me the purse," Drew commanded, and he grabbed the handle and yanked on it, just as the study door flew open.

"Janet!"

Janet couldn't believe it. Ian rushed into the room. Deputy Vaughn followed a step behind him. "Back off and put your hands where I can see them!" Ian yelled at Drew.

Was she seeing things? Was that really Ian? What was he doing here? She was so relieved she wanted to collapse, but she wasn't sure she could trust her eyes.

"I said for you to back off." Ian's voice was low, guttural. The metal badge on his police uniform glinted in the overhead light.

Drew slowly pulled back and put his hands in the air.

"Step away from the women," Ian said. Drew took a tentative step back.

"I tried to stop them, Drew." Gina was a few steps behind Ian and the deputy. "They jumped the fence and barged their way in. I told them they couldn't come—"

"That's enough, Gina," Drew said. He either didn't want to hear more or was cautioning her not to say more. In any case, she closed her mouth abruptly.

Ian folded his arms across his chest. "You're going to explain why I caught you manhandling my wife, and after that, you're going to tell the full story about that missing briefcase and everything you've done over the years to cover it up."

Drew didn't say anything. He seemed stunned. But he couldn't possibly be as stunned as Janet was. How had Ian found them? What was he doing here? How had he managed to show up just at the right time?

"I'll get these women safely out of here, and then we can talk," Ian said.

"I don't have to do anything you say." Drew's tone was defiant. His hands were still in the air, but his tone indicated he was not surrendering. "They brought those negatives into my house. I don't have to let them take them out."

Janet held up her phone. "Even if you take the negatives, that doesn't get rid of the recordings of this conversation," she said. "It's all right here, where you basically admit we're right about what your father did."

Drew lunged at Janet.

His face, screwed up in anger, was the last thing she saw before everything went black.

CHAPTER TWENTY-NINE

"Here's another cup of coffee." Veronica put a paper cup into Janet's hands.

"Thank you." The coffee was bitter and tasted like motor oil, but it was hot and somehow comforting, and it might keep her from falling asleep sitting in the hard plastic chair. Debbie was already home in bed, and Ian had promised they could go home soon. He needed to finish the paperwork after his mad dash to Cleveland and his dramatic rescue.

On the long drive home, Janet and Debbie sat in the back of the police cruiser while Deputy Vaughn drove Debbie's car. Ian explained how he came out of the interrogation room and Veronica told him Janet wanted to talk with him right away. She also told him that Janet had been acting strangely. Ian explained that he called three times, and when Janet didn't pick up, he used the locator app to see where she was. When he realized she was halfway to Cleveland, he figured out what she was up to. He asked Captain Hernandez to continue the robbery interrogation, grabbed Deputy Vaughn, and followed after them, sirens blazing, covering the distance in half the time it should have taken them.

Janet was so grateful, and so glad no one had gotten hurt. Well, not seriously, anyway. She had a lump on her head and a headache from being knocked over when Drew came for her. But the shock of actually harming her had jolted Drew, and he'd surrendered peacefully.

Janet knew she'd messed up. She knew she'd pulled Ian away from a suspect interrogation. She knew she'd put herself and Debbie in danger. She understood that they had been foolish to confront Drew themselves instead of waiting for Ian to turn his attention to the evidence they had presented, as he surely would have eventually.

Still, Janet couldn't help but feel a little bit pleased that he'd come to her rescue. That he'd abandoned everything to save her. She hadn't done what she'd done to try to get his attention, and if she could go back, she would do things differently, but still…

"Are you ready?"

She looked up. Ian stood in the doorway. He was still as handsome in his uniform as he had been the first time she'd seen him wearing it all those years ago.

"You don't need to continue interrogating your suspect?"

"Hernandez got him to confess. He's behind bars, where he belongs."

"In that case, yes, please."

Janet stood, and Veronica took her coffee cup. Janet hoped she was heading home soon too. She had to be exhausted. Janet took Ian's hand and followed him out of the office and down the stairs to his car.

"Thank you," she said as she buckled herself in. "And I'm sorry."

Ian put the car in gear. "I'm just glad you're all right."

"I am, because of you."

Ian looked straight ahead. His face was silhouetted against the dark night by a streetlamp. "I would never let anything happen to you. I would never get over it."

The words warmed something inside her.

"And I'm sorry that I made you feel that your case wasn't important," he continued. "I know that's why you felt like you had to take matters into your own hands."

Even though it didn't excuse what she had done, it was still gratifying to hear him say it.

"I'm sorry I acted irrationally," Janet said. "And that I didn't show that I trust you to keep your word. I know you would have investigated Drew eventually. I know the case you were working on was important."

"It was important. And, in retrospect, I wish I had told you the reason I had to prioritize the cases the way I did. Smollen didn't just take money from the liquor store. He held the owner and two customers at gunpoint when he did it. He got away, and we didn't know what he would do. We only knew he was armed and dangerous. It was imperative that we find him as soon as possible. I couldn't bear the thought that you might be in danger. That's the real reason I was so focused on that case."

"Smollen? You mean Curtis?"

Ian nodded. "I know you went to talk to him a couple of times." He gave her a look that said they'd talk about that later. "That's why I was worried you would be danger. There has always been a personal connection for every robbery for him, and I worried that you had put yourself in danger by getting on his radar."

"I'm sorry I acted so foolishly," Janet said again.

"And I'm sorry I didn't listen to you," Ian said. "The fact that I was working on a high-profile case does not excuse the fact that I didn't take what you said seriously." He took a deep breath and let it out slowly. "And you were right, in the end. The recording you made makes it clear what you suspected was true—Guy Master took that money. That's going to be a big story."

"Hopefully it will lead to the Master family finally doing the right thing."

"They can't fix history," Ian said. "But they sure can write some big checks to make up for it now."

"Just think of all the good that can be done with that money."

Ian nodded. "And just think of how many lives can be changed now that the truth has been revealed."

Janet looked over at her handsome husband, and in that moment, she knew she was the luckiest woman alive.

CHAPTER THIRTY

O kay, everyone, Dad just texted that they're on their way," Janet said. "They should be here in a few minutes."

She looked around the café, which had been transformed for the surprise anniversary party. Streamers and balloons and vases of fresh flowers gave the space a festive atmosphere. The replacement photo had been hung, and now that they knew the significance of that picture, it was even more special to Janet and Debbie. On the far wall was a banner that said HAPPY 50TH ANNIVERSARY and was signed by everyone in attendance.

Debbie was there with her parents, and many of their friends from church had come out as well. Patty, Harry, and Greg were all there, along with Paulette and Kim and her husband. Some colleagues from Mom's former publishing job had shown up, as well as a couple of Dad's former accounting clients. It was wonderful to see so many friends come out to celebrate her parents.

"I'll get the lights," Tiffany called out, and dashed toward the switch. It was good to have her home again, and even though she had to return to school tomorrow, she'd be back for Thanksgiving in just a few more days. There were some giggles and whispers as the room dimmed, but they only had to wait a few minutes until headlights swept the parking lot and Dad's car stopped. Car doors opened and closed, and then they heard footsteps.

"There are a lot of cars here," Janet heard Mom say, her voice muffled through the glass.

Janet wanted to kick herself. She should have told everyone to park behind the depot. She hoped that wouldn't give away the surprise.

Their footsteps grew closer, and Janet expected to hear her mom ask why they were at the depot, but she didn't say anything. Then Janet heard the door open, and Dad said, "Take a look," which they'd agreed would be the signal. Tiffany flipped on the lights, and Mom and Dad stood in the doorway while everyone yelled, "Happy anniversary!"

Janet watched her mother's face as she took it all in. Mom was smiling, her eyes wide. She looked delighted. She looked thrilled.

She looked... Well, she didn't look at all surprised.

"Thank you so much for putting this all together," Mom said, turning to Dad. She kissed his cheek. "I know how hard you worked to pull this off, and I'm so grateful."

"Wait," Tiffany said. "What do you mean you know how hard he worked to pull this off? It's a surprise party."

Mom laughed, and then she leaned over and planted another kiss on Dad's cheek.

"I know your grandfather wanted it to be a surprise," she said. "But after fifty years, one thing I've learned about him is that he's terrible at keeping secrets." She squeezed his hand.

"You knew?" Janet asked.

"I knew from the moment he first had the idea," Mom said. "When he left a to-do list by the bed that said, 'Number one. Ask Janet about hosting surprise party.'"

"Dad!" Janet couldn't believe it. How could he have been so careless?

"And then he asked me what kind of food I'd want at a party—"

"You told me you were subtle about that!" Janet said.

Dad smiled sheepishly. "I didn't say what it was for."

"And he asked me for contact information for all of our friends," Mom continued.

"I didn't have everyone's email addresses," Dad said. "What was I supposed to do?"

"And I overheard him inviting Tiffany to the party," Mom continued.

"You did hear that!" Tiffany laughed. "I was wondering what Grandpa was doing."

"I didn't think she could hear me," Dad said, shaking his head. "She was watching *Wheel of Fortune*. She gets completely absorbed in that show."

"Did anything else give it away?" Janet was laughing now too. Her poor dad looked shocked, but he was smiling.

"Oh yes. Let's see. He took his suit to the dry cleaners. He hasn't done that since he stopped working. He's been a nervous nelly all week, and I've caught him whispering to himself at least half a dozen times in the past few days." She smiled at Dad. "Your big speech is going to be beautiful, by the way. Then he told me to dress up tonight but wouldn't say where we were going. Do you want me to go on?"

By this point, everyone in the room was laughing. It was not exactly how Janet had expected the party to start, but it ended up being better. Ian stepped up next to Janet and put his arm around her waist. She relaxed against him and let her head rest against his shoulder.

"Let me be clear that the fact that I knew about the surprise does not diminish in any way my gratitude that you went to all this trouble." Mom turned and faced Dad before she continued. "Even if you hadn't been so hilariously bad at this"—Dad laughed again, as did most everyone at the party—"after fifty years of marriage, I don't think you could keep a secret from me in any case. We know everything about each other—our habits, our beliefs, our preferences—and I wouldn't have it any other way. I love you, Steve."

Dad leaned down and gave Mom a kiss. "I love you too, Lorilee. I didn't think it was possible to love you more than I did on our wedding day, but over the years I've found that I love you more every single day."

"Happy anniversary," Mom said, and then turned back to the gathered crowd. "Now let's all enjoy this party I've heard so much about."

As everyone laughed and started talking and mingling, Janet held on to Ian.

"I love you more each day too," he said quietly.

"I was about to say the same thing." Janet knew how rare it was to still be married to the man she loved after so many years. She'd been blessed. They'd both been blessed. God had given their marriage His favor, and she hoped that, by His grace, they would make it to fifty years as well.

For now, though, she was content to stand here surrounded by people she loved, holding on to her husband. She knew that, come what may, she'd be holding on to him for the rest of her life.

Dear Reader:

When I began researching the history of the Dennison depot, I came across some amazing pictures of the station and the people who made it so special during World War II, and I was intrigued by the idea of locating the clue to an old mystery within an old photograph. The picture I describe in this book is made up, but I had so much fun creating the details and setup for the photograph as well as imagining how it was possible for the money to vanish with so many people around.

The idea of using a misfiring cannon for the high school's rendition of "The 1812 Overture" is credited to my dad, who loves classical music and has a particular fondness for that piece, and also to my mom, who watches the Boston Pops perform it in the famed bandshell every Fourth of July, complete with military cannons being fired over the Charles River. Even though the origins of that piece of music have nothing to do with America, it will always feel patriotic to me.

I also had fun thinking about Janet's mom and dad's fiftieth anniversary party. My own parents will be celebrating their fiftieth soon. It seems like an impossibly long time to be married to me, and it's an incredible achievement. I know how lucky I am to have been raised by parents in a stable marriage, and now that I've been married a while, I realize how much hard work it must have taken for them to make it appear easy. I know marriages don't always work out the way we hope they will, and how sometimes marriages fall apart even when we don't want them to. I am grateful for my parents' example and for the ways God has blessed their marriage, and I pray my husband and I will be able to make it to fifty years ourselves someday.

I hope you like reading this book as much as I liked writing it.

Best wishes,

Beth Adams

ABOUT the AUTHOR

Beth Adams lives in Brooklyn, New York, with her husband and two young daughters. When she's not writing, she spends her time cleaning up after two devious cats and trying to find time to read mysteries.

A GLIMPSE of the PAST

Remembrance Day and Poppies

I initially included the detail of the Canteen Girls wearing poppies on their lapels simply as a way to date the historic photograph I wanted to include. I knew that Kim Smith, who, no doubt, was familiar with the history of Armistice Day, would be able to connect the poppies to November 11 immediately, which would allow our sleuths to find the newspaper coverage of the theft quickly. But as I learned more about the poppies, I became intrigued by how they became an international symbol of remembrance for fallen soldiers.

Armistice Day—now called Veterans Day and celebrated on November 11 to mark the end of World War I—is still celebrated in many parts of the world as Remembrance Day. And many people do still wear poppies on Remembrance Day, primarily because of John McCrae's poem "In Flanders Fields" but also due to the work of two indomitable women.

According to the History Channel, an American woman named Moina Michael, a professor of history at the University of Georgia, read "In Flanders Fields" in *Ladies Home Journal* and vowed to wear a red poppy as a sign of remembrance of the sacrifices of the Battle of Ypres, which McRae's poem commemorates.

She came up with the idea of selling silk poppies as a way to raise money to help returning war veterans, and she campaigned to get the poppy recognized as the official US symbol of remembrance.

Across the pond, a French woman named Anna Guérin organized sales of poppies to help rebuild France after the war. She was invited to the UK to speak, and in 1921, the British Legion began selling poppies to raise money to help soldiers. Guérin also spoke at the American Legion about her idea for an "Inter-Allied Poppy Day," and soon after the organization adopted the flower as its symbol of remembrance. Other nations followed suit, and today poppies are worn around the world on November 11 as a symbol of remembrance for fallen soldiers.

In the United States, the tradition has developed a little differently. We celebrate all veterans, living and dead, on November 11, and Memorial Day—which was signed into law in 1971—is the day we mourn the soldiers we've lost in battle. In many places in the country, you can still find people wearing red poppies on Memorial Day, all because of the work of these two dauntless women.

FROM the HOME-FRONT KITCHEN

Janet's Pumpkin Waffles

Ingredients:

2 large eggs

¾ cup milk

¼ cup melted butter

1½ teaspoons vanilla

¾ cup canned pumpkin

1 cup all-purpose flour

1 tablespoon baking powder

1½ teaspoons granulated sugar

¼ teaspoon salt

1 teaspoon cinnamon

½ teaspoon nutmeg

Nonstick cooking spray

Optional for serving—butter,
  maple syrup, powdered
  sugar, whipped cream,
  chopped pecans

Directions:

Preheat a waffle iron while preparing the batter. In a large mixing bowl, beat eggs and milk and then stir in melted butter and vanilla. Add the pumpkin and stir until smooth. In a separate bowl, mix flour, baking powder, sugar, salt, cinnamon, and nutmeg. Add dry ingredients to wet and stir just to combine. Do not overmix.

When the waffle iron is hot, spray with nonstick cooking spray and pour in enough batter to go most of the way to the edge. Cook until crisp and brown. Serve with maple syrup or other toppings and enjoy!

Read on for a sneak peek of another exciting book
in the Whistle Stop Café Mysteries series!

LET IT SNOW

BY BECKY MELBY

Balancing two boxes of Christmas decorations in her arms, Debbie Albright walked down the front steps of the craftsman-style house she'd lived in for the last six months, and then she turned back to admire her handiwork. After an already restless night filled with too many memories, she'd been startled awake by sirens and crawled out of bed long before the first-day-of-December sun's rays had seeped through the curtains.

While sipping a cup of reheated gingerbread-spiced mocha latte and listening to Christmas carols, she'd decked a grapevine wreath with sprigs of holly, pinecones, and a smattering of bright red berries, finishing it off with a big, cheery buffalo plaid bow. As she studied the wreath from the sidewalk, she smiled a bit brighter and cheerier than she actually felt and then straightened her shoulders and lifted her chin. This *would* be a good Christmas. And by the time she finished decorating, here and at work, all doubts about calling Dennison home again would vanish.

Wouldn't they?

With a wistful sigh, she continued her short walk to work, breathing in the crisp morning air as she reflected on past holiday seasons here in her hometown. Dennison, Ohio, did Christmas well. And now she was part of making that happen.

As she approached the train depot that housed the Whistle Stop Café, which she owned and operated with her longtime best friend Janet Shaw, she scrolled through her mental checklist of the day's chores. "Change the Flavor of the Day on the chalkboard from gingerbread spice to roasted chestnut, put up the tree, order more—"

Her words faltered on a whoosh of breath that crystallized in midair. Something was missing. Beneath the arched trusses supporting the depot roof, a large empty space of dark red brick gaped like a toothless smile. The brick surrounding the space had faded with time, making the empty spot more pronounced.

The wooden bench, scarred with names and dates carved over eight decades, was gone. "How? Who would—"

"Where's the bench?" Janet's stunned voice joined hers. She hadn't even heard her come out of the café.

"I have no idea. It was here when we left yesterday. Wasn't it?"

"Yes, I'm sure it was." Janet's brow creased over her hazel eyes dimming with confusion. She shook her head. "We would have noticed if it was gone. *Someone* would have."

"Maybe the village had it sent out to be refinished or repaired or something. Kim will know." Kim Smith, curator of the depot museum, was also on the village board.

"Terrible timing if they did."

"I know." The idea of the bench being "sent out" for anything had sounded lame when she suggested it. The old oak bench had to weigh well over a hundred pounds, and it had been bolted to the concrete. Any needed maintenance could be done much more easily right where it was. And, as Janet had just pointed out, the timing would be awful.

"Who does it actually belong to anyway?"

"Um…" Debbie stared at her friend. "I'm not sure. It would have been the property of the Pennsylvania Railroad at one time. But the village owns the depot, so I imagine 'we the people' own the bench."

The sound of car tires crunching gravel made them turn in tandem. Kim got out, holding a giant cardboard box. "Morning! What are you two—Where's the bench?"

"You don't know?" Debbie felt the stir of uneasiness she'd awakened with returning.

"No clue."

Kim took her keys out of her purse, and the jingle broke the quiet. "Let's get ready for the day and start making phone calls. I'll call the president of the village board. If he doesn't know, I'll call the mayor. It's not like someone would just up and steal it in the middle of the night. Right?" She turned to Janet and Debbie for confirmation, but all she got in return was a weak smile from Janet and a shrug from Debbie.

A dim light bulb flickered in the back of Debbie's mind. A memory from many years earlier. "I'll call my mother. She wrote to me once about a couple of women who were in a heated debate about the bench. One thought it was an eyesore, and the other said it was an icon of Dennison history." Debbie had lived an hour and a half north, in Cleveland, from the time she'd started college until she'd moved back in June. Every week for twenty-five years her mother had sent a newsy letter, first by snail mail and then email, chock-full of town gossip. "Either of you remember that?"

Kim and Janet both shook their heads. "I've been working here for twenty years," Kim said, "and I don't remember hearing about it."

"It's a long shot. The women might already be gone, but it's a place to start."

Kim opened the door, and they entered, all three stopping to scan the inside of the depot as if sharing the same thought. Was anything else missing?

Debbie's gaze swept from the marred plank floor to the vaulted ceiling of the depot's waiting area, refurbished to replicate the way it would have appeared during the heyday of the railroad. She looked at the familiar artifacts from days gone by. The original depot clock, its face yellowed but still keeping perfect time. Several rusty lanterns, some with yellow glass, some with red, the kind that would have been swung to tell trains to slow or stop.

Pulling out her own keys, Debbie opened the door to the café. She scanned the space that had seemed to call her name back in the spring when the idea of reopening the old café first came to her. From the wood flooring to bright yellow walls and white pressed-tin ceiling. She stepped over to the antique cash register, set the boxes down, and stared up at the black-and-white photograph of a group of women standing behind a rolling cart filled with small paper bags. In front of them was a sign that read THE SALVATION ARMY CANTEEN. FREE SERVICE TO SERVICE PERSONNEL.

Everything appeared to be in order. Nothing to do now but start the day. And pray. *Lord, help us figure this out. Soon.*

"We need that bench," Janet said, echoing the thoughts in Debbie's head.

"I know." Debbie sighed as she reached for a pink candy-cane-print apron. "We spent more money than we should have on those postcards." She walked to the counter and picked up a glossy card displaying a photograph of a smiling couple sitting on the iconic—and now missing—bench. Two small children in footy pajamas snuggled on their laps, apple cheeks rosy as they smiled. The caption read, *Come have your picture taken in front of the Dennison Depot, enjoy a fresh-from-the-oven treat at the Whistle Stop Café, then ride the Dennison Christmas Train!*

Janet tapped her finger on the card. "I don't think it's a coincidence that these cards went out three days ago."

Debbie's shoulders fell. This was not the way to start the season she was determined to make merry and bright. "I don't want to agree with you, and we won't know until we've made those calls, but I think you're right." She glanced out the front window. "It's no coincidence."

"I can't remember. That was over twenty years ago." Becca Albright, Debbie's mother, leaned her elbows on the café counter as she sipped a cup of roasted chestnut coffee sweetened with a dollop of maple syrup. On her way to her part-time receptionist job, she wore a black cardigan over a crisp white blouse and black pants. A glittery green Christmas tree pin softened the severity of her professional attire. She squinted at her daughter. "You look tired, sweetie."

"I woke up too early," Debbie said. She turned to Janet. "Did you hear the sirens?"

"Ian was called out before dawn. All I know is there was an accident out on Stillwater."

"Oh!"

Debbie raised an eyebrow at her mother's sudden exclamation. "It was Rita Carson and Doris Kimball." She shrugged. "Your dad always teases me about the way my brain connects dots. 'Stillwater' reminded me of the summer I spent in Stillwater, Minnesota, with my grandparents when I was little and met my cousins who lived in Kimball, Minnesota. And that made me think of Doris Kimball. Anyway, those two almost split the town in half over the depot bench back in…must have been 1999. I've never since seen such a fierce debate at a town meeting. You remember Doris, right?"

Debbie nodded as she unpacked a box of bright red mugs she'd ordered just for the season. "Of course." Doris Kimball had played a major role in fostering Debbie's love of reading. "She was the stereotypical librarian. And Sunday school teacher. Very kind, but very serious. She still is. And even in retirement she doesn't talk over a whisper. I can't picture her involved in a heated debate."

"She sure came out of her shell during that meeting. The council president had to use his gavel a couple of times just to break up the argument. I guess her passion overcame her shyness."

"I have much more vivid memories of Mrs. Carson." Debbie still felt a twinge of fear when she thought of the stern-faced fifth-grade teacher. "They called her 'the warden.' Do you remember how terrified I was before I found out I'd be in Mrs. Stebinski's room?"

Her mother laughed. "You threatened to run away, as I recall."

"No one wanted to be in her class. She was mean. I can definitely imagine her raising a ruckus about the bench. But why? Why did it matter so much to her?"

"I know. I always wondered that myself. I think there was something going on that none of us knew about."

"Hmm." Debbie rinsed a red cup then dried it and hung it on a wrought-iron mug tree she'd found in the storeroom. "I think—" She stopped when Kim hurried into the café, the look on her face saying she couldn't wait to share something.

"Morning, Becca. Sorry to interrupt. I talked to three village board members. The board didn't order moving the bench. I also talked to the mayor. She has a theory. *Ohio Heritage* magazine is doing a contest for cities with a population under five thousand in their online issue this month. They're sending out reporters and photographers to take pictures of 'nostalgic Christmas scenes' in the five towns that got the most nominations, and then they'll ask their followers to vote on the one that best depicts 'The Heart of Ohio at Christmas.' Dennison is one of the five!"

"Seriously?" Debbie looked at Janet, who was adding apple fritters to the display case but clearly listening. "We nominated Dennison in that contest back in July. So did quite a few of our regular customers. The nomination form called for a paragraph and a picture. Several people said they were going to send their Christmas portraits taken on the bench. I think Janet even gave them a list of adjectives and phrases to use like 'nostalgic,' 'cozy,' 'heartwarming,' and 'true Christmas spirit.'"

Janet scurried over. "Dennison made the list? That's huge. *Ohio Heritage* has thousands of subscribers. For Dennison to make the top five means that many more people than just our customers nominated us."

Kim nodded. "Their reporter and photographer are coming here on December sixteenth. They want pictures of the depot and train, and they specifically mentioned the bench. We have to find it before then."

Debbie frowned. "So…you said the mayor had a theory. Is she thinking one of the other towns is trying to sabotage our chances of winning?"

"That's exactly what she's thinking."

"So we need that list," Janet said.

Kim rolled her shoulders, a sure sign that tension was building. "That's a problem. They aren't publishing the list. No one is supposed to know what towns they've chosen until their holiday issue comes out."

"But someone knows." Debbie stepped behind the counter and picked up the latest print edition of the magazine. Every month, she and Janet took turns paging through *Ohio Heritage* when the café wasn't busy. "Where is this published?" She opened the front cover and perused the tiny print on the first page until she found the address. "Coshocton."

"That's only forty-five minutes away," Kim said.

"Home of the Roscoe Barbeque Company," Janet said. "I'm thinking we might need to take a drive after we close this afternoon." Her eyes twinkled. It was no secret that Janet loved good barbecue.

Debbie grinned. "I'm in." The restaurant, located in Historic Roscoe Village, had the best smoked brisket she'd ever tasted. The

Village, a recreated nineteenth-century canal town, offered self-guided living history tours, inviting visitors to interact with the town's doctor, printer, weaver, blacksmith, and broom maker. Taking a short road trip might be just what she needed to get out of her head for a bit. "Think they'll give us the list if we show up at their office?"

"Probably not," Kim said. "But if you give them a picture of the bench, maybe they'll send it out to their photographers across the state and ask them to keep an eye out for it. Though I can't believe anyone would be so brazen as to have it out where it can be seen. I'm thinking it's probably well hidden somewhere."

The bell above the café door jingled, and Harry Franklin, one of Dennison's oldest residents, shuffled in, leaning on the arm of his granddaughter, Patricia. Crosby, the depot's trusty four-legged mascot, trotted in behind them.

"Where is my bench?" Harry's uncharacteristically gruff voice carried across the café. Harry was a porter at the depot during World War II and then a train conductor for years after that. He was retired now, and much of his day was spent sitting on the depot bench. If anyone had a right to call it his, Debbie supposed it would be him.

The black-and-white dog who lived with Harry and followed him everywhere looked up with a dejected expression in his big brown eyes, as if to echo Harry's question. Crosby spent as much time at that bench as his owner did.

"We don't know what happened to it, but we're hoping to find out." Debbie motioned to Harry's favorite table, right in front of the window. "Maybe you can help us solve the mystery." She stepped past him and pulled out the chair facing the tracks.

WHISTLE STOP CAFÉ MYSTERIES

Patricia took the chair across from her grandfather. "We'll each have a cinnamon roll. Hold the calories in mine."

Debbie smiled. "Two fresh-from-the-oven cinnamon rolls, one sans calories, coming right up." She turned on her heel. She didn't need to ask what they wanted to drink. Unadulterated black coffee for Harry. He often said, "Like it was back in the day when the pot sat on the woodstove from morning to night. Loved that last cup of the day." Peppermint mocha for his granddaughter.

As Debbie filled their mugs behind the counter, she whispered to Janet, "Think I'll go join them for a bit."

"Good idea." Janet opened a drawer and took out a pen and the notebook they used for a running list of things they needed to order. "Take notes. I'll heat up their cinnamon rolls."

Debbie tucked pen and notebook in her apron pocket and carried two red mugs to the table. "Mind if I join you?" she asked.

"Not at all," Harry said, pointing to the chair next to Patricia.

Debbie sat and then pulled out the notebook. "We have no idea who took the bench. You know everyone in town, Harry. We need a list of suspects. Who do—"

"You aren't going to need that. We don't need a list. Only one name to write down. There's only one person I know foolish enough and strong enough to take my bench."

**While you are waiting for the next fascinating story
in the Whistle Stop Café Mysteries, check out
some other Guideposts mystery series!**

SAVANNAH SECRETS

Welcome to Savannah, Georgia, a picture-perfect Southern city
known for its manicured parks, moss-covered oaks, and antebellum
architecture. Walk down one of the cobblestone streets, and you'll
come upon Magnolia Investigations. It is here where two friends
have joined forces to unravel some of Savannah's deepest secrets.
Tag along as clues are exposed, red herrings discarded, and thrilling
surprises revealed. Find inspiration in the special bond between
Meredith Bellefontaine and Julia Foley. Cheer the friends on as they
listen to their hearts and rely on their faith to solve each new case
that comes their way.

The Hidden Gate
A Fallen Petal
Double Trouble
Whispering Bells
Where Time Stood Still
The Weight of Years
Willful Transgressions

Season's Meetings
Southern Fried Secrets
The Greatest of These
Patterns of Deception
The Waving Girl
Beneath a Dragon Moon
Garden Variety Crimes
Meant for Good
A Bone to Pick
Honeybees & Legacies
True Grits
Sapphire Secret
Jingle Bell Heist
Buried Secrets
A Puzzle of Pearls
Facing the Facts
Resurrecting Trouble
Forever and a Day

MYSTERIES of MARTHA'S VINEYARD

Priscilla Latham Grant has inherited a lighthouse! So with not much more than a strong will and a sore heart, the recent widow says goodbye to her lifelong Kansas home and heads to the quaint and historic island of Martha's Vineyard, Massachusetts. There, she comes face-to-face with adventures, which include her trusty canine friend, Jake, three delightful cousins she didn't know she had, and Gerald O'Bannon, a handsome Coast Guard captain—plus head-scratching mysteries that crop up with surprising regularity.

A Light in the Darkness
Like a Fish Out of Water
Adrift
Maiden of the Mist
Making Waves
Don't Rock the Boat
A Port in the Storm
Thicker Than Water
Swept Away
Bridge Over Troubled Waters
Smoke on the Water
Shifting Sands
Shark Bait
Seascape in Shadows

Storm Tide
Water Flows Uphill
Catch of the Day
Beyond the Sea
Wider Than an Ocean
Sheeps Passing in the Night
Sail Away Home
Waves of Doubt
Lifeline
Flotsam & Jetsam
Just Over the Horizon

MIRACLES & MYSTERIES of MERCY HOSPITAL

Four talented women from very different walks of life witness the miracles happening around them at Mercy Hospital and soon become fast friends. Join Joy Atkins, Evelyn Perry, Anne Mabry, and Shirley Bashore as, together, they solve the puzzling mysteries that arise at this Charleston, South Carolina, historic hospital— rumored to be under the protection of a guardian angel. Come along as our quartet of faithful friends solve mysteries, stumble upon a few of the hospital's hidden and forgotten passageways, and discover historical treasures along the way! This fast-paced series is filled with inspiration, adventure, mystery, delightful humor, and loads of Southern charm!

Where Mercy Begins
Prescription for Mystery
Angels Watching Over Me
A Change of Art
Conscious Decisions
Surrounded by Mercy
Broken Bonds
Mercy's Healing
To Heal a Heart

A Cross to Bear

Merciful Secrecy

Sunken Hopes

Hair Today, Gone Tomorrow

Pain Relief

Redeemed by Mercy

A Genius Solution

A Hard Pill to Swallow

Ill at Ease

'Twas the Clue Before Christmas

A NOTE FROM the EDITORS

We hope you enjoyed another exciting volume in the Whistle Stop Café Mysteries series, published by Guideposts. For over seventy-five years, Guideposts, a nonprofit organization, has been driven by a vision of a world filled with hope. We aspire to be the voice of a trusted friend, a friend who makes you feel more hopeful and connected.

By making a purchase from Guideposts, you join our community in touching millions of lives, inspiring them to believe that all things are possible through faith, hope, and prayer. Your continued support allows us to provide uplifting resources to those in need. Whether through our communities, websites, apps, or publications, we inspire our audiences, bring them together, and comfort, uplift, entertain, and guide them. Visit us at guideposts.org to learn more.

We would love to hear from you. Write us at Guideposts, P.O. Box 5815, Harlan, Iowa 51593 or call us at (800) 932-2145. Did you love *Fools Rush In*? Leave a review for this product on guideposts .org/shop. Your feedback helps others in our community find relevant products.

Find inspiration, find faith, find Guideposts.

Shop our best sellers and favorites at

guideposts.org/shop

Or scan the QR code to go directly to our Shop

Find more inspiring stories in these best-loved Guideposts fiction series!

Mysteries of Lancaster County

Follow the Classen sisters as they unravel clues and uncover hidden secrets in Mysteries of Lancaster County. As you get to know these women and their friends, you'll see how God brings each of them together for a fresh start in life.

Secrets of Wayfarers Inn

Retired schoolteachers find themselves owners of an old warehouse-turned-inn that is filled with hidden passages, buried secrets, and stunning surprises that will set them on a course to puzzling mysteries from the Underground Railroad.

Tearoom Mysteries Series

Mix one stately Victorian home, a charming lakeside town in Maine, and two adventurous cousins with a passion for tea and hospitality. Add a large scoop of intriguing mystery, and sprinkle generously with faith, family, and friends, and you have the recipe for *Tearoom Mysteries*.

Ordinary Women of the Bible

Richly imagined stories—based on facts from the Bible—have all the plot twists and suspense of a great mystery, while bringing you fascinating insights on what it was like to be a woman living in the ancient world.

To learn more about these books, visit Guideposts.org/Shop